SIGNS IN THE CITY

SIGNS IN THE CITY

Colin Marchant

HODDER & STOUGHTON
LONDON SYDNEY AUCKLAND TORONTO

British Library Cataloguing in Publication Data

Marchant, Colin
    Signs in the city.
    1. City churches—Great Britain
    I. Title
    274.l   BV637

ISBN 0-340-37426-8

CONTENTS

FOREWORD

by David Sheppard, the Bishop of Liverpool

Colin Marchant issues an invitation to a pilgrimage of understanding about the Inner City and its life. He is a trustworthy guide, with the experience of twenty years' ministry in West Ham under his belt. He and I shared in that pilgrimage, when for several years our time in East London overlapped, as I served in the next district of Canning Town at the Mayflower Family Centre. I learned a lot from Colin Marchant then; I find there is much to learn from *Signs in the City*.

The book has much to say to suburban, town and rural Christians; it provides a source book for many to begin their own pilgrimage of understanding of the Inner City. That will not lead very far, unless they are willing to give the Inner City a much higher priority in their thoughts and actions. That includes acknowledging that, like it or not, we are members one of another in one nation and one Church. There is a destructive poverty and lack of opportunity which tramples on people's God-given gifts in the Inner City; that is the dark side of the prosperity and good opportunities which so many people experience in Britain.

The invitation to pilgrimage will mean looking at our daily life over again – work, politics, life style. Those who travel into great cities to work have been described as the "gatekeepers"; they are the gatekeepers who open or close the gate to opportunities, to jobs, to promotion, to good services being provided for those who are so often powerless to make their voices heard.

It will mean looking with fresh insight at the Bible; Colin Marchant rightly says that we have often evaded the plain meaning of scripture. We have turned the message of God's kingly reign breaking into the whole of life into a private, spiritualised churchy handbook. As he says, the Bible is full of Justice and Peace as God's purpose for the whole world. Poverty is not tolerated in the Bible; it causes concern, anger and protest.

Signs in the City is a "both . . . and . . ." book. There is a most damaging division between Christians who will pose evangelism and social justice as though they are opposites. Here is a book in which is firmly embedded a deep belief that Christ can both change people from inside out *and* reform society so that it better reflects the Kingdom of God.

The invitation to pilgrimage will mean learning new priorities for the Church to which we belong. Like Colin Marchant I believe my years in East London were the greatest education of my life; he shares with you some of the Signs in the City which God has used to enrich his life – people's realism and directness, the sense of history in sharing in "the economic, racial and social struggles, which echo the experience of so many of the world's population."

He shares with us what it means to learn from energetic and encouraging Christians; there are not so many of them, for there are few fringe members, who are just there for the look of it. Christians, who have been brought up to withdraw from the risk of getting their hands dirty in the world, will see a great challenge in the "earthiness and the eternity" which Colin Marchant sees in West Ham. If they stay on the pilgrimage, they will learn much more than they dreamed of the word made flesh, who still dwells among us.

1

JOURNEY IN

A PERSONAL PILGRIMAGE

The Woolwich Ferry began it. That short journey across the Thames on the old-fashioned boats was a boyhood treat. Standing on the deck I peered with my suburban eyes at the dense housing and industrial skyline of London's dockland at Silvertown. I never left the known security of the boat. I always returned without getting off. I saw, but I did not see. I was too young.

Covent Garden continued it. In my teens and twenties I travelled daily from the suburbs to Central London. The North Kent Line carried me from Erith in Kent to my first job as a packing boy in the old Covent Garden market. On my journey I noted the change from open fields to dense housing; from suburban gardens to the backs of terraced housing. Each day Plumstead station marked the start of an almost unbroken slab of visual grayness that ran on through Charlton, Deptford and Bermondsey to London Bridge. I saw, but I did not see. I was too busy.

My journeys began in the suburbs. I had no option for I was born, raised and educated there. The attitudes and values of the area were accepted and absorbed. My own identity, life-style and opinions were the products of a Baptist, middle class home where education was very important, the "Protestant work ethic" was embraced, "getting on" was encouraged and personal talents were valued. Church going, and the road to personal faith, were inextricably woven into the pattern. This was the way, and I walked in it.

Covent Garden market woke me up. Three months after starting work as a packing boy in 1946 in the old fruit and vegetable market I decided to go to the Annual Harvest Festival Service. It was held in the market church of St. Pauls, hemmed in by the stacks of fruit boxes, potato bags and waiting lorries. I arrived early and found a vantage point on the back row to watch the arrival of the congregation. Twelve came. All wearing suits. A handful of salesmen and office workers. Not a single porter, warehouseman or lorry driver. The contents of that service have long since disappeared from memory but the consequences have gone powerfully on. It was almost a vision. A sudden, frightening glimpse of a cultural chasm – and I stood then fairly and squarely on one side.

The first stages of this deeper, inner journey were all set in or around London. Covent Garden was followed by Kings Cross. A year's pre-college pastoral experience in Kings Cross introduced me directly to the struggles and questions of the inner city, made me notice how church members almost automatically moved out to the suburbs such as Finchley and that the leaders travelled back every Sunday to a district to which they had become alien. Four years of theological training for the Baptist ministry followed in Spurgeon's College – perched on a hill overlooking London and, like most of our theological colleges, physically removed from the roots of the inner city. During that time I worked in a student-pastorate on a new housing estate at Oxhey, near Watford. This was a London County Council overspill estate where I worked with a group of young people whose parting gifts of books were each pointedly inscribed with the words, "Towards bridging the gulf."

The Midlands gave me another push. I lived in a council flat overlooking the giant B.M.C. car-making complex at Longbridge in Birmingham. On that vast housing estate wages at that time were high, industrial relations low and the Church pitifully weak in numbers. The Welfare State had been in operation for ten years and the William Temple College (then at Rugby) launched a social survey which included my "parish". Uncertain and unwilling, convinced my task was only to make converts and build up the Church, I was abruptly confronted with a living, human profile of the roads and the flats. One in four homes had "unmet needs". Under the title *Responsibility in the Welfare State* the researchers probed beneath the superficial well-being of the late 1950s to reach the hidden personal and social problems so often exacerbated by lack of resources. In the midst of affluence lurked poverty and struggle.

Four years in Luton in a central church again revealed the centrifugal force that sends Christians spinning away to the outlying areas while still wistfully returning to their "home" church. During this time I lived in an area where the first wave of West Indians were settling and slowly taking over whole streets. The continuing outward movement of the white members and the rapid inward stream of the black Christians created an uneasy co-existence both in the church and the neighbourhood.

A LEARNING EXPERIENCE

But it is East London that has most vividly spelt out the urban realities for me. In 1965 I came to West Ham to be the minister of the Baptist Church that had produced the West Ham Central Mission, a network of caring agencies. A church once boasting 1,000 members in the 1930s had known decades of erosion. The accepted equation known to sociologists as "religious lift" is simple:

"Become A Christian =To Get On = To Get Out".

It was certainly illustrated in the churches of East London. Much of the lay leadership travelled in from the suburbs and the congregation did not mirror the district. For twenty years I have been a part of a living, loving and lively congregation struggling with urban mission. In the church we have seen some young couples deciding to reverse the tide and to stay. We have struggled with a wide variety of evangelism approaches, taken part in changing ministry patterns (solo, team, shared) and watched the style of worship move from the formal to the open and participating.

In 1970 we moved as a family across the road from the Baptist Manse into a community/residential centre called Lawrence Hall to continue our ministry. Here we live in an urban maelstrom. 3,000 people a week share in the many clubs, the Children's Centre, political groups, Churches and leisure activities that use our premises. Here people dance, eat meals, sing, think, buy jumble, start groups, drink coffee... and worship. Seventy people live in Lawrence Hall, mainly older people in sheltered housing with some young couples here for two years before they plant themselves in the district. As a family we have journeyed in. Here we have settled and here we belong. Here our children have grown up.

East London has given us a direct, first hand experience of inner city life. For twenty years we have watched the changes, enjoyed the local spontaneity and warmth, struggled with fundamental issues like education and unemployment. We have shared in many experiments – both in Church life and in the community structures of Lawrence Hall opening up into the wider spheres of social services, health and advice. Within all this has gone the mental wrestling that has dragged me into the worlds of sociology, comparative religion and theology; asking searching questions about faith and attitudes. It has been a fascinating, sometimes painful journey.

FELLOW TRAVELLERS

My travelling is not unique. I have become aware of other people journeying. Many have been travelling out, away from the inner city. There has been a mass exodus of the achievers, those with educational qualifications or personal drive, and prominent among them have been the Christians. In London the flight is always outwards, away through the suburbs to the Home Counties and even – like lemmings! – to the coast.

But others have been journeying in. They have come

looking for work, a home, or a refuge. From the Caribbean they have come to drive our buses and staff our hospitals. Asian people expelled from Uganda or arriving directly from Bangladesh have opened their shops and started home industries. And still they come from Britain – Belfast, Birmingham or Glasgow – believing that there is work, opportunity, or a hiding place in East London.

It feels a little like living in a wash-basin with the plug out and both taps on. Gurgling out of the plug-hole go those buying houses in the suburbs or moving to better jobs – they have "made it". One of the taps is the visibly obvious stream of Commonwealth immigrants who have come here to live and work. The other is the constant flow of white people arriving to live with relatives or friends and hopeful of work.

This urban turmoil is far wider than the U.K. After fourteen years of immersion in the Church and community life of East London a series of opportunities took me to the U.S.A., Asia, Australia and Europe.

A Churchill Fellowship on the Rehabilitation of the Inner Cities took me to Chicago, Detroit, Philadelphia, New York and Washington in the U.S.A.; the Consultation on World Evangelisation (1980) in Thailand had a workshop on "The Urban Poor"; I spent a month in Australia with urban mission agencies in Melbourne and Sydney; and in 1984 I shared in the European Baptist Congress at Hamburg under the theme "Seek the Welfare of the City". Everywhere I went I met the same concerns and questions about the urban dilemma. I also identified very different, but complementary, groups of people. At one level, local or indigenous groups were staying instead of moving; facing instead of ignoring; banding together instead of going it alone. They were being joined by the "incomers", people coming to stand alongside the indigenous; translating their concern into action, choosing to live and to work in the inner cities, bringing their convictions and their expertise. These two groups are the fellow-travellers I have met and with whom I work. They are to me signs of hope and agents of the Kingdom. With them I have learnt many lessons and faced many issues.

But now I am very much aware of another group. Fast-growing and widespread, they have been alerted by the media, and awakened by the evidence of the indigenous or the report of the incomers. These are the concerned and the perplexed. Whenever I journey I meet them. They come up after I have spoken in a suburban church, they cluster around in our colleges, they ask for the literature. They too have begun a journey. If I have written for any group I have written for them . . . for you? All I can do is to record, comment and interpret what I have seen and learnt.

REASONS AND MOTIVES

This book is written in the belief that what is happening in the cities and urban centres of our country has great significance for us all. There are strong reasons that call for a listening and a learning. These include:

- The fact that the U.K. *has the highest percentage of urban population in the world*. The Economic and Political Year *World View 1985*[1] has a World Table that includes Urban population for 1980 in percentages. With 91% the U.K. tops the league of nations.
- The reality of the *symptoms and stresses of the inner city spreading steadily and inexorably outwards* to the next ring of neighbourhoods or being decanted to the overspill estates.
- The knowledge that all this is *created by long-standing national policies and attitudes* in which we all share.
- The truth that *decisions are made by people outside the areas concerned*. Many suburban people, often those whose family roots were once in the inner city, make judgements and have influence over the lives of those still there.
- The realisation that we are in *danger of becoming two nations* geographically, politically, socially, economically, culturally and religiously.
- The awareness that the urban poor situation in the

U.K. is a *microcosm of the world pattern*. The gap between rich and poor, the meeting and mingling of the races, the impact of new technology on traditional values – all these world features are focussed for us in our inner cities.

While these are all good reasons why we should be concerned about the inner cities and housing estates there are some deeper motives which apply directly and pointedly to Christians. They have to do with Gospel mandates and the nature of the Kingdom of God:

- From the standpoint of *evangelism* the inner cities present us with the most intractable missionary situation in the U.K. For over 100 years all the indices of faith in the inner cities have been one third of the national figures. In spite of all the efforts and initiatives, that position remains the same today.
- Seen from the viewpoint of *caring* the whole Church knows that where human need is greatest we are at our weakest. There is so much to be done and so few to do it.
- In the perspective of the *Kingdom Of God* we know that the great biblical themes of wholeness, justice and freedom are very far from the experience of the people of the inner cities.

Taken together the reasons compel attention and the motives impel towards action. That attention and that action does not take place in a vacuum. There is already a deafening and continual barrage of signals reaching us from the inner cities and housing estates.

CONTRASTING SIGNALS

If you tune in to the signals you will receive conflicting messages. Signals of distress are interspersed with signs of hope. The initial, mounting and insistent signals are those of stress. These are visual in the bleak environment, verbal through the graffiti, and physical in the violence.

Bitterness surfaces in the racism, impotence in unemployment and resentment at poverty. Professional people feel overwhelmed, politicians speak of powerlessness or confrontation, and the locally-born struggle to escape or alternatively sink into apathy.

But there are other signs: signals of hope, indications of the Kingdom, and evidence of the Spirit. They run from personal presence to national concern; they include new churches and the Archbishop's Commission on Urban Priority Areas; they emerge in fresh approaches in evangelism and effort in social transformation; they are expressed in the renewal of the traditional and the springing up of the contemporary. Something is happening.

AN INVITATION

I want to invite you to join in a pilgrimage of understanding. Put on one side the misconceptions and myths. Step by step enter into the experience and feelings of those who both enjoy and endure the realities of life in the city. Take in the deepening questions of our society. Check out the themes and insights of urban faith with your own scriptural convictions.

In this book you will be asked to look at the surface features and the underlying roots of urban life. You will glimpse the effort Christians have made to "make the Word flesh" in the past. You will be called to hear and to heed today's stress signals of deprivation, poverty, division, powerlessness and confusion. Then, out of the stirrings and shakings that have so radically affected society and the Church will emerge the signs of hope.

The struggles that surround these signs will be closely examined and this will bring you face to face with some of the underlying questions that lurk beneath the social and spiritual turmoil of the city. Finally, you will be able to see some of the ways ahead and be given some help for the journey.

But all this will be only words and an exercise in futility

unless and until we can really enter in, and respond, to the cry of the urban people:

> When we have really understood the actual plight of our contemporaries, when we have heard their cry of anguish, and when we have understood why they won't have anything to do with our "disembodied" Gospel, when we have shared their sufferings, both physical and spiritual, in their despair and their desolation, when we have become one with the people of our own nation and of the universal Church, as Moses and Jeremiah were one with their own people, as Jesus identified Himself with the wandering crowds, "sheep without a shepherd" *then* we shall be able to proclaim the Word of God – but not till then.[2]

2

BEGINNING TO UNDERSTAND

THE CONTEMPORARY KALEIDOSCOPE

The kaleidoscope is a children's toy that has lasted. The mirror reflects the continual shifting and rearrangement of the same pieces. There they are, caught in the restrictions of a frame and thrown about by the shake of an external hand. They settle down, only to be violently jerked into uncertainty and crisis. Whenever you look there is a different constellation. However you look there are the same components.

Within the urban kaleidoscope are the pieces we label housing, family life, work, education and environment. They can be isolated but they are always part of an overall pattern. Touch one and you touch all. They are linked but separate.

You begin to understand when you look closely at the ingredients that mix together to make up the urban reality. Look at the headlines and stories of a local paper. In just one edition our weekly tabloid spelt out deprivation, violence, run-down and racism.

Deprivation in:	"School to Close"
	"Hypothermia Tragedy"
	"Hospital Beds Crisis"
Violence depicted:	"Gang's Terror Arson"
	"Cashier Knifed"
	"Bank Con"
	"Rape Suspect"

Run-down expressed: "Post Office Axings to go ahead"
                          "Docks plan no good for locals"
                          "M.P. calls on council to break
                              law"

Racism emerging: "Race Eviction"
                          "The Nazi Connection"
                          "Lawmen in hate note enquiry"

But the punchy, dramatised journalistic presentation only tells part of the story. The hidden stories are not told. We rarely glimpse the response, the effort and the commitment of those who face and grapple with the urban forces. A closer look at some of the key pieces in the contemporary kaleidoscope helps to bring understanding.

HOUSING – RONAN POINT

Ronan Point, one of 123 tower blocks in Newham, is both a local landmark and an international symbol. It replaced the tight-knit rows of terraced housing built for the incoming dockers and industrial workers during the 1880–1900 population explosion. They were swept away by the combination of war-time blitz and peace-time planning. The new "street in the sky" immediately cut neighbourhood ties and created acute social problems.

In 1968, I was awakened by the sound of emergency vehicles travelling past our home. When I arrived at the foot of Ronan Point the cause of the jagged hole high up in the building was not known. Two of our older Church members lived there and I went with them to pack a suitcase as the towerblock was evacuated. Later I returned to stand with the silent crowds. A week afterwards I buried one of the victims.

Since Ronan Point is just down the road I watched the reconstruction, knew the fears of returning tenants, and heard of the final verdict of structural insecurity. In 1984 the block was evacuated and abandoned.

Here, for me, is an inescapable, ever-present symbol of the significance of housing. In that one building is carried the story of human needs, social change, broken hopes and personal frustration. Focussed here are the dilemmas of local authority planning, national policy and family needs.

In 1977, nearly 1.8 million people lived in 450,000 high-rise flats in Britain, all of them built since 1953 – 92 % of these dwellings were built in large towns and cities. Within each tower block is a cluster of pressures – shortage of land, the power of the planners, the new-technology dreams of the architects, and the building industry investment in pre-fabricated methods.

The truth is that whole sections of our community will never be able to buy their own homes and have little choice about where they will live. Options narrow as private landlords disappear, council waiting lists lengthen and financial cut-backs slow down new housing.

Young people wanting to stay in the inner city face acute difficulty in acquiring council housing, see a decreasing (and expensive) supply of private lets, and often face a creeping gentrification in which the higher purchasing power of incoming buyers overwhelms the resources of the poorer-paid local people.

Even plans designed to ease pressure – Housing Benefits, Fair Rents, Tenants Protection – end up by confusing tenants and restricting choice. Add to this the social effects of tower blocks, the wholesale break-up of communities by redevelopment, the competing claims of host communties and immigrants, and the central position of housing as a key to the inner city problem becomes clear.

It is an ever-present segment of the urban kaleidoscope. Home is a place to live, a base camp for life, a family centre and an accepted essential. Yet in 1982/3 our local council statistics showed that the monthly average of fifty-nine families rehoused from the waiting list was swamped by the 239 families who joined the list. Furthermore, only one in ten of the houses let had a garden. In this one London Borough 26,000 dwellings are substandard and 14,000 lack basic amenities such as an inside toilet or bathroom.

Within the statistics are the people. I know a road sweeper who retired to discover that his landlady insisted on him leaving his rented room at his old work hours. One day I discovered him huddled on a seat outside the post office: that experience pushed me into the world of housing associations and sheltered housing. I know a young couple who spent the first year of their marriage apart – then made their first home together in a double flat at Lawrence Hall.

The people suffer frustration and impotence, as expressed in this local paper report:

Sky flat families went on the march last week armed with banners – and a song sheet. The Christmas Carol "Silent Night" suddenly became "Silent Strife, Tenant's Life". And even the Beatles would have been proud of this one:

Oh, you'll never get to heaven (echo)
In a council flat
Cos a council flat
Ain't where its at.

Oh, you'll never get to heaven
On a council scheme
Cos a council scheme
Is just a dream.

FAMILY LIFE – THE FAMILY CENTRE

Inside the homes a struggle is in progress. On one side, couples rooted in a strong marriage bring up their children, watch over ageing parents with the weekly visit, support neighbours in need, and share in the local network of knowledge and care. On the other side, the breakdown of the extended family group which gave support and identity, the effects of wholesale redevelopment, the economic pressures of unemployment, the questioning of authority, and the clash of cultural

attitudes, particularly among Asian families – all combine
to threaten and sometimes to break up family life.

The story of ten years' work among under-fives here in
Plaistow shows the changing emphases. It all began with
a playgroup at our church to encourage small children to
form relationships and to express themselves before going
to school. A Young Wives Group and a Mothers and
Toddlers Club rapidly followed as the needs of mothers
surfaced – extended family ties were weakening and
questions about child-rearing were growing. An Opportunity Group that faced the problems of families with a
handicapped child grew up alongside the playgroup.
Then, as financial pressures grew and more mothers were
compelled to work, the network moved into full-day care
in co-operation with the Social Services. A help-line
telephone service for parents unable to cope with the
emotional demands of children was added as social
pressures mounted.

Later, visits to homes at Christmas in 1982 revealed
poverty and an inability to cope and led to the establishing
of a Family Centre (with G.L.C. funding) to befriend and
support parents struggling with an increasing wave of
difficulties that included housing, money and relationships. Finally the Women's Project, with public funding,
was launched alongside the other groups to assist women
to find employment through the acquisition of job-skills.

That is one story in one place, illustrating both the
pressures bearing down on family life and one local
response.

WORK – COMMUNITY INDUSTRY

A place to live, family life – and a job. These are the three
basic and accepted ingredients for a full, secure human
life. An unemployed person lacks status, influence and
identity, inside and outside the home and family.

The inner city has known a long process of attrition and
obsolescence. Industrial pull-out and the shift from
manufacturing to service industries have gone alongside

the national economic recession. Increasing educational standards at 'O' and 'A' level have put inner city young people at a disadvantage in the competition for jobs. The rising percentage of women at work has changed the employment pattern. "If you want to be out of work, be black, male, a teenager and live in East London" may be cynical but is too near the mark for comfort.

Behind the graphs and the statistics are the human hurts. I know men with no history of heart disease who, soon after redundancy, have heart attacks. The "induced cardiacs" of older men remove them from the frustration of job hunting and give shared justification for inactivity to both family and father: "He'd like to work but he can't because he's got a bad heart now." At another level is the experience of one black girl: in the diary she showed me was the neat, bleak recording of twenty-two applications or interviews ending with the cryptic comment, "Never heard anything."

We have one of the Manpower Services Commission schemes in our community centre. Run by Community Industry, it offers a year's work-experience to a group of black and white teenagers in our children's centres, reception, Volunteer Bureau and painting schemes. One or two go on to find work but the majority "drop off the conveyor-belt" into a void. I think of Joan, a gentle, quiet West Indian girl who came to the end of her time without any work. We urged her to link up with a local centre, gave her names and addresses – but she disappeared. Too shy to take the initiative, too depressed to try again, she retreated into the hidden security of her family.

People without work respond in different ways. Some become resigned and stay-at-home. Others find money through the "black economy" as they decorate homes, do nights on petrol pumps or drive mini-cabs without declaring their incomes. The rise in prostitution and the increase in thieving ("winning" in local parlance) have roots in unemployment and take women and men into the arenas of law-breaking and crime.

Yet many persist in the daily visit to the Job Centre, the

weekly look-through of the adverts in the local paper, the hopeful visit to factories, the request to family and friends to "put in a word for me" and the acceptance of under-paid, unsatisfying work. And all the time there is the feeling that the sudden closure of a factory (lack of profitability), the disappearance of offices (relocation), the cut-back in the work-force (over-manning), the refusal to replace retiring employees (redeployment) and the con-traction of traditional industries (automation and com-puterisation) are all due to hidden forces shaking and disrupting the known and familiar. Whether it be massive multi-nationals, impersonal bureaucracies, the economic climate, political decisions or technical revolution, the reaction is the same – something, somewhere has the power to uproot a personal job-skill, abruptly shift employment patterns or empty a busy factory. And apparently no one can halt the shaking process or predict the consequences for those caught up within the employ-ment piece of the urban kaleidoscope.

This has become the central economic issue for the U.K. and the exercises in "job creation" by Government schemes fail to grapple with the scale and entrenched nature of the problem. The gap between the unemploy-ment total of 3.3 million and the advertised vacancies of 142,000 is a sharp pointer to the national dimensions of the problem. The more personal, debilitating effects on the individuals are known to us at first hand – and they hurt.

EDUCATION – NEWHAM EDUCATION CONCERN

In our early days in West Ham a regular Sunday night youth group known as "The Melting Pot" met in our home. It was made up of lively young East Londoners who were struggling to hold together their new found faith and what was happening all round them. They focussed on education, joined forces with a teacher who had chosen to return to her home district after moving out (that was very unusual then!) and suddenly they found themselves plunged into a disturbing and exciting adventure.

They discovered that our Borough was 121st out of 122 local education authorities in the league table of further education. They decided to challenge the way parents and teachers accepted the situation. Other people joined in. The needs and the concern were local and real. Out of this group sprang Newham Education Concern. I attended the public meetings, heard about the lobbying, and saw the results of the pressure groups. Out of this activity sprang the Parents' Centre. Ten years on their Annual Report indicates the scope of the struggle for education in the inner city. Adult literacy, employment consortium, crisis counselling, community resources, holiday schemes, career support, under fives, home and school, run alongside community publishing, information and re-search, and the Education Shop. Eleven full time staff and a budget of £105,000 are required to carry through this borough-wide programme.

The 1981 Census and a report from the Department of Education and Science in 1982 record some frightening statistics about the children in our London Borough.

29 % come from "low-income" socio-economic groups.
18 % live in households without their own bath or inside W.C.
35 % are from families of New Commonwealth origin.
61 % live in over-crowded accommodation.
15 % live in households containing at least one unemployed adult.

It is not surprising that many of Newham's children have low educational aspirations, poor motivation and do not achieve their full potential.

Added to this, our libraries have the lowest rate of lending issue per head out of thirty-two London boroughs. We have the third lowest level in London of residents with professional or higher educational quali-fications. And a high ethnic population and cultural diversity require special lessons to meet the different needs.

The problem is recognised by the Government. Nine of Newham's fifteen Secondary Schools and fifty-six of the ninety-three Primary Schools are designated Social Priority Schools. Newham, of course, is but one of the cities and boroughs in the U.K. wrestling with the educational dilemma.

The problems of education in industrial areas is compounded by the arrival of the non-English speaking children, fragmented by the intention of cultural groups to educate their children in their own way (whether that be the old-established Church schools, the controversial Muslim schools or the new Christian schools) and accentuated by the way the great majority of teachers (as all professions) live outside the area in which they work. Add to these the reorganisation of Comprehensive Schools, the emergence of Community Schools, the debate about the nature and purpose of education and cut-backs in resources and the scene is set for yet another of the shake-ups and shifts in pattern which are so marked a feature of the urban kaleidoscope.

There are more deeply personal questions. Parents ask whether they should put their children at risk by an inner city education. This applies to those able to leave the situation as well as to those considering a move in. I can only react in two ways to this often-expressed quandary. The first comes out of our personal experience, the second is a matter of principle.

All three of our children have been educated in the inner city passing from Primary to Comprehensive Schools – and all three have gone on to further education. In this experience we have learnt three things:

- Local attitudes to education are either dismissive or adulatory.
- Middle class education for working class kids does not work. We begin from different sides and rarely meet in the classroom.

- Education is the way up and out. Those who could shift attitudes, argue from experience or create new approaches are the very people who move physically and mentally away from their own culture.

Beneath the personal experience lies the far more important principle – that education of all children is and must be a fundamental concern for us all. The education of our own children is only one aspect. Education concerns the future of individuals and society. To be blunt, all children matter.

ENVIRONMENT – MANOR ROAD ADVENTURE PLAYGROUND

As you drive into the inner cities the first impression is that of a sea of housing stretching in all directions. Dilapidated streets, shared homes, tower blocks, terraced housing and council estates form a continuum of bricks and concrete.

Within this sea are the jutting rocks of industrial presence in the factories, railway lines, docks and warehouses that initially drew the workers but now linger on to remind of past days. Now the derelict sheds, disused yards, and "to let" signs provide silent reminders of past prosperity and changing technology.

All this is set in a visual bleakness where dense housing in close proximity to commercial buildings is rarely relieved by play-space or leisure facilities and is often blighted by vandalism, graffiti and litter.

It is easy to itemise the legacy of environmental and physical problems:

- Cheaply built working class housing which is now badly in need of renewal.
- Housing developed in too close proximity to bad industries.
- Dense development with low levels of provision of open space, parks and playing fields.
- Victorian and Edwardian industrial and commercial

buildings unsuited to modern manufacturing, without room to expand or adapt.
- Street patterns better suited to the horse than cars and lorries.

This legacy has been compounded by:

- Vandalism, damage, dumping and littering.
- Large areas of unsightly, vacant, derelict or damaged land and buildings.
- Traffic congestion and the impact of busy trunk roads cutting through the area.

The Manor Road area of West Ham can be paralleled in hundreds of industrial districts. It is bounded by railway lines, a main sewer outfall, a cemetery and main roads. It was there a group of us set up an Adventure Playground. With a local committee and a strong leader we tried to create space for play and relationships. We learnt a lot. Damage to the buildings, anger from the neighbours, raids by the police and difficulties over funding led to the wind-down and closure. But the need remains and the pressures persist.

But the episode of the Adventure Playground taught me that something, however little, can be done. Goodwill and resources are available and an impact can be made. The worker at the Playground met with the leader of the local authority, housing associations renovated old buildings, a tenant's association was formed and a physical transformation took place. Whenever I become oppressed by the apparent impotence of groups working in the inner city I go back to Manor Road and remember all that happened there.

But the effects of the environment must not be discounted. After we have taken our holidays in the spaciousness of the Yorkshire Moors or the green villages of southern England the return home is almost a physical impact. There is a closing in, a chaotic untidyness and an underlying backcloth of noise. Perspectives, colours and sky-areas all change. In spite (and sometimes because) of all the efforts of planners and political authorities the environment remains a constant visual pressure that bears down and conditions. The able escape to the suburbs or the countryside. Families who stay create an insulated home-life supported by an active policy of D.I.Y. decorating and an apathetic acceptance of all that is outside!

INNER CITY AND OUTER ESTATE

These are the features of life in the inner city. But they are now just as true for the housing estates. These communities were built mainly in the 1950s and 1960s on the periphery of big cities to house families being moved out from the inner slums. Many are now towns in their own right. A report by an independent urban research centre in 1984 concluded that they have become Britain's "forgotten area of deprivation" with unemployment running at three times the national average. About two million people live on these estates, mainly in the north of England and Scotland. With little or no special Government help these outer estates are worse off than the inner cities.

Geographically the urban poor of the U.K. are concentrated in the great conurbations of Merseyside, Manchester, Tyneside, the West Midlands and London; they live in cities like Nottingham, Bristol, Glasgow and Belfast; and can be found in unexpected places like Bath or Brighton.

They are rooted in the traditional working-class areas or flung out into vast housing estates like Dagenham or Kirby. Their homes back on to the railway lines of Cardiff or soar up in the tower blocks of Sheffield.

The majority still live in the areas of older industry – clothing and textiles, shipbuilding and docks, steel and cars. These are the areas of poor housing; a mixture of old Victorian terraces and modern council houses. These are the areas with high concentrations of manual workers, stricken by industrial decline and lack of opportunity.

Many are perched on the new housing estates that ring the cities or spring up in surprise in the countryside. Some of these are huge – like Wythenshawe within Greater Manchester and Dagenham within Greater London, each with a population of 90,000.

Inner city people and residents of housing estates are often linked by the consequences of the planning process and share similar attitudes.

The endless sprawl of the conurbations or the concrete jungle of the new estates has to be focussed to be understood. We have to see and to hear. We need to look and listen. Then we have to look beneath the surface.

3
BENEATH THE SURFACE

GNARLED ROOTS

Beneath the surface of the urban kaleidoscope are old and tenacious roots. They are long-lasting, stretching back to the Industrial Revolution and beyond that to the mediaeval class system. They are exceptionally tough, having defied massive efforts to change them by the Churches, charities, political parties, Government intervention and wholesale planning. They are matted, hard to untangle, interlocked, and constantly thrusting out. The roots have an inner unity and a perplexing diversity. They penetrate international and national policies and derive their life from personal and structural sin.

Individuals sense the grip and influence of these roots and struggle to escape them. But they are so strong because they are anchored in the past, penetrate the whole of human life and seem to be outside the command of those most affected by them. We are not dealing with a new phenomenon which has emerged in the last decade. We face a desperately familiar scenario with some new features sharpening and accelerating the situation.

SET IN HISTORY

Between the 1830s and the 1930s stands the 100 years in which Britain experienced urban concentration and urban diffusion. In the period between the Reform Act and that of the great inter-war depression, towns and their suburbs grew up, expanded and later interlocked. In 1831, 34 % of the total population in the U.K. lived in local authority areas classified as urban; by 1931 that was true of 80 % of the population.

Millions of people moved from the countryside to the industrial towns. A process based upon education, income, skills and influence separated the working class from the middle class and ultimately created the monochrome one-class areas of the inner city.

Initial rapid growth slowed down and imperceptibly changed to population stagnation, followed by decline and decay. Successive waves of immigrants coming from Europe in the 1930s, the Caribbean in the 1950s and the Asian sub-continent in the 1960s have underlined the problem and made visible the process.

The inner city problems did not begin with the riots of 1981. They have been with us for more than a century. *The Bitter Cry of Outcast London* was written by W.C. Preston in 1883 for the London Congregational Union as "An inquiry into the conditions of the abject poor." The twenty-page pamphlet was written in a mood of strong emotion and anger to publicise appalling living conditions. In 1889 Charles Booth began his massive survey *Life and Labour of the People in London*[1] and took seventeen years to compile the seventeen volumes of detailed facts and evidence on poverty, industry and religious influences. The *Daily News' Census* in 1902/3 which surveyed the religious life of London concluded that the "majority of the inhabitants remain, owing to either indifference or hostility, uninfluenced and unrooted" by religion.

When I first came to live in West Ham in 1965 I realised that neither my suburban upbringing nor my pastoral experience in Birmingham and Luton had "coded" me to understand the East London situation. For months I sat in the reference library reading the faded pages of the local newspapers. I worked through all the books written in or about East London. I talked to many of the old people in the district. Slowly I built up a picture of long-standing forces deep-set in the area's history which had first created and then continued to shape this society. No one can fully understand the complex roots of the inner city until they see today's reality as the latest step in a long drawn-out chapter of urban history which is as yet unfinished.

SHAPED BY ECONOMY

It was the need for money that drew labourers to the mines, factories and docks. It was the profit motive that attracted money and allocated its use. Now the inner city faces the reverse procedure under the bland modern phraseology of "capital outflow," "economic disinvestment," "runaway capital" and "red-lining". Whatever the language used there is no hiding from the fact that it is the economy that shapes.

Politicians of all parties agree. Peter Shore, then Labour Secretary of State for the Environment, commented in 1977: "I am in no doubt that the problems faced by the inner urban areas are of a most serious kind . . . The causes lie in their relative economic decline, in a major migration of people, often the most skilled, and in a massive reduction in the jobs which are left."[2]

Peter Walker, when Conservative Secretary of State for the Environment in 1972 said: "In our approach to the environment, we have endeavoured in the first two years under the new D of E to make a switch of resources to bad areas."

Both parties united in the G.L.C. book, *London, We're staying here:* "The inner areas are essentially communities built in the late 19th and in the early part of the 20th century around a nucleus of thriving industrial and commercial centres from which the industrial life-blood has now drained away leaving behind a residue of multiple social problems that can only be resolved through economic regeneration."

The draining away of life from the inner cities suddenly accelerated in 1979. The economic crisis that began then has delivered a double blow at the least advantaged of our society. It is a crisis that has sharply increased inequality as well as curtailing the creation of real wealth. Three factors affect the urban poor:

- The long-term weakening of the manufacturing industries and their displacement from markets at home and abroad.
- A particularly severe trade cycle slump since 1979, pulling output down by over 15 %.
- The adjustment of products and processes to the new technologies which is socially painful.

These economic factors have brought about unemployment and relative poverty on a hitherto unknown scale to a high proportion of the population.

In 1979 *The Guardian* published an Economic Extra under the title "Is there any hope for the inner city?" and summed up with:

> The main cause of Inner Area unemployment is not the collapse of the economy of Inner Areas but the fact that Inner Areas have for 150 years or more been the areas in which those most vulnerable to unemployment live. Impose on that an aggregate level of unemployment that has been as an upward and steadily rising trend since the mid-1950s and you perceive Inner Area unemployment.[3]

The predicament of the urban poor is not unique to the industrial areas of the U.K. The Coalition of Urban Bishops of the Episcopal Church in the U.S.A. sharply pointed to the shaping power of the economy in their book *To Hear and to Heed* when they said:

> By economic, political and social design, cities have become the enclaves of the poor and working people who live under the constant threat of poverty. There is evidence pointing to the existence of an underclass defined by such factors as race, economic status,

language, culture and age which results from the
functioning of our economic system and, indeed, may
be necessary to it.[4]

The concluding words "... which results from the
functioning of our economic system and, indeed, may be
necessary to it" have haunted me ever since I read them in
the U.S.A. and looked back over the Atlantic to my own
country asking if the words fitted. I now believe they do.

EXTERNALLY CONTROLLED

Historical processes and economic forces are, by their very
nature, impersonal. But they are personalised when the
levers of power are seen to be in the hands of people living
outside the inner cities. So traditional folklore and
contemporary experience fuse together in a "them and us"
philosophy. An unseen and anonymous "them" are
believed to make decisions and wield power over the
visible and known "us".

This external control is evident at many levels. There is
the imposition of structures – whether political, social or
religious. There is the way financial aid is funnelled
through Government programmes or an elite of inner-city
based agencies.

Urban structures or organisations have been imposed
arbitrarily upon an unwilling or unknowing population.
Two examples in East London illustrate this. In the
industrial sphere it was the Metropolitan (Noxious
Industries) Act of 1859 that compelled unpleasant
industries like chemicals, oil processing or soap-making
to move out of London into neighbouring boroughs
without consultation or referral to the local council. In the
ecclesiastical world, the Anglican churches of West Ham
have been in four dioceses – London, Rochester, St. Albans
and Chelmsford – and in 1875 the local paper commented:
"We confess that we are not exactly pleased at the manner
in which West Ham is handed over from one Bishopric to
another, and that without any tangible benefits."

Decision-makers are often outside the area. Leadership is imported, whether it be the directors of local authority departments (few of whom ever live in the inner city) or in the Church appointments (so often appearing to be arbitrary and without consultation). This elitist view of leadership was expressed by the founder of the Dockland Settlements when he looked back on the way public schools and universities became involved in the Settlement movement: "The church, very wisely, felt that a first appeal for help should be made to the younger, and more fortunate generations. So to the Public Schools of England the appeal went."[5]

The Church is no different. Clerical domination is rooted in the concept of the centrality of the professional ministry, the English historical acceptance of the parson (the person) as the accepted community leader, and the advantages of a university education which had always characterised the Anglican clergy and eventually the Free Church minister. This autocratic paternalism nurtured dependency within the Churches, relegated lay helpers to an inferior status, and made the establishment of working class leadership a virtual impossibility.

Then there is financial oversight. British economic philosophy has meant that the relief of financial hardship is accompanied by a sense of loss of dignity. Direct financial aid to individuals and indirect monetary influences through the funding of social agencies flow in from the outside. Parliamentary debates on Housing Benefits, rate-capping and the future of the Metropolitan Boroughs yet again spell out that decisions taken at Westminster touch the pocket of individuals and determine the policies and even the existence of local authorities concerned with urban poverty.

Beneath the surface, the deeply-rooted layers of history have been pummelled into shape by the inexorable pressures of the economy which have apparently been controlled by people who do not live within, do not understand, and are not accountable to the millions of people who make up that part of the British population known as the urban poor.

These are the basic causes, the greatest roots, which lead on to consequences that include the experience of urban deprivation, the creation of the urban poor, the existence of two nations and the "Power and Powerlessness" syndrome. They lie beneath the surface but constantly influence and shape the surface. In a garden the life of the plant depends upon the hidden roots. In the city the seen realities of life are shaped by the hidden forces of history, economics and power.

4

MAKING THE WORD FLESH

Where does the Church stand in this urban process? How have we made the Word flesh?

A journey in can lead to the beginnings of understanding and a closer look can dig away beneath the surface. But I am a Christian with a faith centred on a living God who operates in this world, who has made Himself known through Jesus Christ, and who is continually at work through His Spirit and His people, the Church. Through my own experience and out of my own research I have found myself caught up in the long struggle of Christians to "make the Word flesh" in part of East London.

The themes and illustrations are drawn from the area I know best but I have discovered that they fit elsewhere. Within regional variations, all the motifs and struggles are to be found in all the inner cities of the U.K.

Christians in West Ham have worked away at "making the Word flesh" through the medium of buildings, the visible practices of religion, the efforts of evangelism, the wider issues of social caring, the stress on personal morality, and alongside politics.

This chapter is a "bird's eye view" of the past efforts. It is a story of experiment and struggle, of success and failure, of vision and blindness. It is a survey of where we have been.

THROUGH BUILDINGS

In an urban society, buildings carry messages. The church

is no exception. Spires and towers, vicarages and halls, community centres and cathedrals – all are symbols set visibly and vividly in urban space.

In places like West Ham the pre-urbanisation symbols were the great *abbeys* and the network of Parish Churches. Two Abbeys symbolised control as they rose dominant and powerful at Barking and Stratford Langthorne. The *parish churches* were a sign of the centrality of faith. In and around them roads converged, schools were built, halls were erected and the "rites of passage" reminded individuals of the centrality of the church in their lives while the liturgical cycle depicted the divine control of time.

The industrial invasion, followed by the rapid build-up of population, created a greater social complexity and a wider range of human needs.

Missions are the ad hoc answer as relief, entertainment, education and worship all took place in hastily erected buildings. Under the umbrella of Mission marched a great variety of approaches ranging from powerful "empires" with a large staff to the tiny tin-roof back street Mission Hall. Whether the dominant theme was evangelism, pastoral care or social action the message of the Mission was that of concern.

But most *chapels*, whether Free Church or Catholic, were erected by congregations for their own use and local people saw them as worship, teaching or fellowship centres for denominational purposes. Within these congregations the commitments of membership, high standards of personal morality and shared beliefs created a gathered community who believed themselves (and were considered) to be different from the wider society.

The fenced-in, solidly built Chapels spoke of differences. This message was confirmed by the way Free Church members who moved often continued to return to their church from a distance and so widened the gap between the local and the gathered community.

The growing realisation that the assumed centrality of the Parish Church was little more than a pious hope, that

Missions grew away from their evangelistic ethos and that
the Chapels were distant and different from the surround-
ing population led to new approaches by Christians
towards the close of the nineteenth century. The twin
emphases of personal evangelism and social caring were
then drawn together by the *halls* of the Salvation Army,
the City Missions and the Methodists.

This visible blending of Parish Church, Chapels,
Missions and Halls has been augmented in the post-war
era by the growth of community centres, and House
Churches. *Community centres* have often replaced the
old-style Settlements and have an open-door approach
inviting participation and partnership. Over against them
stand the *shop-front* and *house churches* with their stress
on smaller, more spontaneous, often charismatic cells of
Christians engaged in evangelism. These have now been
joined by a wave of *Black Churches* using their own
houses and then taking over halls.

Clear evidence of changing religious patterns in the
inner cities is expressed in buildings when *synagogues*
close as the Jewish Community moves to the suburbs, and
mosques and temples open to meet the need of Muslims,
Sikhs, Hindus and Buddhists.

But still the primary local Christian impression comes
through the buildings that set out to "make the Word
flesh" and carry a variety of silent but visual messages to
those who pass by them. That is why the closure, change of
usage, adaptation or questioning of the function of
church buildings arouses such emotion, both within and
outside the congregation.

IN THE PRACTICE OF RELIGION

Within the buildings the worship and witness, rites and
rituals, and prayers and programmes of believing people
have coalesced in the "practice of religion". Church
attendance has always been regarded as the most obvious,
and primary, yard-stick of religious practice.

In 1902 the survey *Life and Labour of the People of
London* commented that:

The great section of the population, which passes by the name of the working classes, lying socially between the lower middle class and the poor, remains, as a whole, outside of all religious bodies, whether organised as churches or as missions, and as those of them who do join any church become almost indistinguishable from the class with which they then mix, the change that has come about is not so much *of* as *out* of the class to which they have belonged. The bulk of the regular wage-earning class still remain untouched, except that their children attend Sunday School.[1]

Nothing this century has occurred to modify that judgement and the literature written, the research undertaken and the experiments carried out all confirm the view that religious practice is at its weakest, whatever criterion is used, in the inner urban areas of England or the vast council estates so closely linked to them.

Yet in 1851 national Census figures showed 44% of the people of West Ham at church on a given Sunday over against a national average of 36%. Churchgoers then were divided into Church of England (65%), Non-Conformist (25%) and Catholics (10%). By 1903 the whole scene had changed dramatically as industry and close-packed housing covered the marshlands and the population jumped from 18,817 in 1851 to 267,358. *The Daily News Religious Census* of 1903 revealed that only 20% of London's population were in church and that West Ham was next to bottom of the borough list confirming that areas like West Ham had then, and still have to this day, church attendances of one-third of the national average. The 1903 figures also showed changes in composition as the Non-Conformists with 56% had overtaken the Anglican 32%, and the Catholics now had 12% of church attenders.

Today the picture has changed again, against a background of a dropping population, industrial decline and a pluralistic society. Only 5% worship God on Sundays and now the Catholics with 3% are easily the strongest section with Asian religions (Budhism,

Hinduism etc.) a growing 1% and the Protestant 1% divided almost equally between the traditional denominations and the new, mainly black churches. Although the incoming ethnic population has reshaped the religious pattern both in numbers and composition the underlying urban process continues. There is a steady decline in religious practice as churches close, attendance drops and influence wanes.

But over against this century-long atrophy must be set the remarkable persistence of religion which continues to survive in the experiments, new methods, life-styles and even superstitions of the urban poor. Yet nothing can hide our failure to win the bulk of the population into the living practice of religion.

The long bleakness is becoming shot through with evidence of new forms of Church life expressed in the church planting, resurrection ministries and alternative models more fully surveyed in chapter five.

BY EVANGELISM

For 130 years social observers, historians and Church leaders have noted the evangelistic intractability of the urban situation. A summary of the 1851 Census pointed out that it "showed that well-tried approaches to the working classes were having little success. It helped church leaders to realise just how solid was resistance to their ministry, especially in the large towns."[2]

In 1971 Nicholas Stacey concluded an intensive five-year period of Anglican team ministry in Woolwich by saying, "I plead guilty to under-estimating massively the depth and significance of social pressures which keep the English working class away from the worshipping community of the Church."[3]

Failure has not been due to lack of effort. In West Ham the records show that the traditional work of parish or gathered congregations was soon supplemented by the Missions, the University or Public School Settlements and a wave of campaigns. Evangelistic movements like the

Salvation Army (1865), Moody and Sankey (1884), the Church Army, The London City Mission and the Pentecostalists moved into West Ham. All shared a concern to reach the "unchurched"; a willingness to use new, often unorthodox, methods; a basis of strong evangelical doctrine; the opportunity for lay people to play key roles; and an immediate initial success which eventually petered out.

Traditional Churches used "bridge" methods. Pleasant Sunday Afternoons and Brotherhoods for men, Women's Meetings and Sunday Schools reached thousands but very few joined the Church itself. Even the post-war Christian Commando Campaigns and the Billy Graham Crusades reached few East Londoners.

A combination of Church weakness and mistaken methods fused with social factors peculiar to the working class to create an impasse. From the Church side, evangelism has too often been indirect, with organisations replacing the "face-to-face" act of witness, non-indigenous, with clergy and imported missioners bearing the responsibility and spasmodic, with occasional bursts of activity assuaging the guilt of neglect. From the non-churchgoer's angle the claims of the Church have appeared to be irrelevant in the midst of the day-to-day struggle for the basic necessities of life; remote, in the different thought-forms, attitudes and activities of the Churches; and non-attractive, in the lack of spontaneity and with the demand for changed standards.

But in the mid 1980s there is increasing evidence that the new life within the Churches and the stress on personal, direct evangelism is beginning to face up to the spiritual emptiness and competing demands of the urban milieu.

VIA SOCIAL ACTION

Church buildings, religious practices, and evangelism have all been set within an arena of social change. The arrival of industry, the in-rush of population and all consequent social history is the story of the struggle with unemployment, poverty, inadequate housing, and population mobility. Christian social action has moved from the tradition of personal charity to the massive network of agencies and programmes that serve many people in a variety of buildings.

It has often been difficult to disentangle social action from evangelism and even harder to see the demarcation lines between caring, reform and political revolution. Opposition has come from evangelical Christians fearing the "Social Gospel" and from local leaders disliking the power and patronage of insensitive Church agencies. Weaknesses include fragmentation of effort, creation of dependency, empire building and the "poultice" approach which tackles symptoms but not causes.

The problem of unemployment relief illustrates both the concern of the Churches and the reaction of recipients. In 1933 soup kitchens, labour yards and relief programmes in West Ham led to a reference to church kitchens where the unemployed "could have a basin of abide with me with tea and rock cake"[4] and a correspondent from the National Unemployed Worker's Movement wrote, "We have no quarrel with the Churches, but we don't accept their theory of pie in the sky when you die. We want the pie while we are still alive."

In spite of the weaknesses the catalogue of Christian social action in areas like West Ham is massive. Provision of education and health facilities, housing programmes and leisure centres, unemployment relief and concern for minorities, hostels for the inadequate and settlements for community activities . . . the list is endless. Even in today's Welfare State the Churches of West Ham are a key component in the social caring network as they work through their community centres, hostels, youth programmes, and action groups. Partnership with statutory authorities, personal pastoral care and individual participation in the political and social structures are all contemporary features.

The positive contributions of this aspect of Christian ministry are those of initiation (district nurses, poor man's lawyer and Darby and Joan Clubs all began in West Ham Church agencies), flexibility, resource gathering and the continual creation of communities of care. The underlying dilemma was known to General Booth who "turned to social reform because he became convinced that poverty itself was a grave impediment to salvation",[5] and left a legacy of uneasy co-existence between the witnessing, evangelising corps and the caring, institutional centres of the Salvation Army.

ALONGSIDE POLITICS

The Churches preferred poultice application to political involvement but the emergence of socialism sharpened the question. The first Labour M.P. in Britain, Keir Hardie, was elected in south West Ham in 1892 and the first Labour controlled council followed in 1898. The old alliance of Tory Church of England and Liberal Nonconformity had been powerful – as in the 1892 election when Anglican vicars graced Tory meetings and Baptist and Methodist Churches were used for Liberal Party meetings but only the occasional Freechurchman or Catholic priest stood with the socialists.

The relationships between the Churches and the forces of socialism have known distinct phases. Initial ambivalence moved through a period of misunderstanding into open hostility – in 1911 Church candidates opposed Labour Party councillors on the issue of the Sunday opening of cinemas! Between the wars an uneasy coexistence was maintained in the face of comments like that of the Bishop of Chelmsford in 1920 that "decay in the Church is co-incident with the rise of labour".[6] Since the last war both sides have been drawn together by their shared experience of decline and their underlying desire to face the accelerating urban problems.

The fringe, but potentially explosive, activities of the present day National Front (the Blackshirts of the 1930s) in an area of high immigration and the revolutionary aims of the extreme left (the communists of the 1930s) in a deprived and powerless district can divert attention from an even deeper political reality for the Churches. That is to be seen in the gulf that grew, and has never been adequately bridged, between the working class political organisations (trade unions, co-operative movement and Labour Party) and the institutional Churches. Only the Roman Catholic Church has really kept a political foothold within the local Labour movement, in spite of individual efforts by the Christians from other denominations.

The long-standing and fundamental uneasiness that many Christians have about party politics has been seriously questioned by the arrival of the new left and the resurgence of the National Front in East London. Can, and should, Christian Churches stand aside from the traumas of political power?

The wave of young Marxists who chose to settle in the inner cities in the sixties and seventies has shaken traditional patterns. The attempted radicalisation of the Labour Party has led to a bitter and continuing struggle between the ensconced, more right-wing socialists and the forces of the new left. This has been reflected in the battles for power in local boroughs and the larger Metropolitan authorities like the G.L.C. In this stormy, U.K. counterpart to the world confrontation Christians have too quickly ignored any partial truth held within the Marxist analysis of the capitalist system because of their dislike of the disruptive tactics employed – or their fear of the disturbing implications. Is there a historical process determining lives? Is the individual to be subjugated to the mass? Should power be held by the few or by the people?

On the other side of the political spectrum, Christians have too often been equivocal or silent about fascist groups like the National Front. This is due to the recognition that the racist views are often a reflection of some strong local white feelings.

During the 1980s more Churches and Christians have begun to share in community politics and a fresh emphasis upon the Kingdom of God has compelled some younger Christians to enter ward parties and to become councillors.

PERSONAL MORALITY

The tests of a "true Christian" were seen in the attitude taken to drink, the use made of Sunday, the disapproval of entertainments, the discipline expected in sex and the refusal to engage in gambling. Unfortunately enjoyment of alcohol, the view that Sunday is a leisure day, interest in entertainments, earthy matter-of-factness in sexual matters and participation in gambling have all character- ised the working class in East London! "Christian" has been linked with "kill-joy" and "thou shalt not" has been the message received.

Positively, the preoccupation with personal morality has maintained biblical ethical attitudes, challenged the slide in moral standards, urged a distinctive style of life, reminded society that social evils are accompanied by victims, and initiated a network of caring agencies. But the Churches have failed to explain the reasons (stewardship, discipline, wholeness) for their attitudes.

An even more serious defect is the evasion by the Churches of the corporate morality involved in economics, war or racism. I found no record of any church meeting in West Ham up to 1975 ever passing a resolution on war or race to match those taken on betting or drinking.

The consequences of this stress on personal morality have been far-reaching. At one end of the spectrum, the Christian Faith has been privatised; at the other, Christians have failed to address issues such as economics and the technological revolution which have shaped our society. We have either initiated or allowed a wholesale process of secularisation which has led to the removal of great slabs of our corporate life (education, health, planning, social services) from biblical insights and the prophetic discipline. At best, we have sustained personal morality in a vacuum; at worst, we have become politically irrelevant.

SOME REASONS FOR FAILURE

With the advantage of hind-sight it is possible to see some
of the reasons why so many of the people in places like
West Ham have failed to hear – or to heed – the Gospel the
Church carries:

- There has been a long-term failure to recognise that the
  urban areas have become mission fields requiring a new
  evangelical urgency and demanding a different form of
  commitment and understanding from members of the
  Church, local or national.
- Our massive investment in social caring has blurred
  the edge of evangelism, presented a one-sided picture of
  the Gospel and often created an enervating dependence.
- The relationship between the Churches and the
  political instruments of the working class (whether
  Labour Party, trade unions or the new left) has often
  been marked with ambivalence and even a mutual
  hostility.
- There has been a cultural and class conflict within the
  Churches themselves which has been seen in the
  dominance of imported leadership, the use of external
  finance which has encouraged both paternalism and
  dependency, and a social manipulation by the more
  articulate and able.
- The Christian preoccupation with personal morality
  has not been matched by an equally powerful concern
  for the wider corporate issues of poverty, war and race.
- The process of secularisation has progressively taken
  from the Church its influence in the wider life of our
  society (as in the sphere of education) and has deeply
  affected the inner thinking of individuals.

The evidence from East London for the workshop on the
Urban Poor at the Consultation on World Evangelisation
in 1980 said:

  The real roots of our failure strike deeper. Within

ourselves we discover an unwillingness to accept fully the pattern of the incarnation (to be and to be among), a refusal to enter into the hurt of our world (the fellowship of Christ's sufferings) and a preoccupation with our own careers and concerns. Even when we set out to serve, or to work with, the people of the inner city we find that our institutions and organisations actually shield us from the painful realities of poverty and divide us from those who are poor.

SOME SIGNS OF HOPE

An analysis is one thing, an answer another. Social change does not stand still and West Ham has now been merged into the London Borough of Newham which has inherited the deeply rooted urban problems and is now embattled by the twin pressures of historical legacy and contemporary economic pressures. In itself it is a microcosm of the urban scene – and was used as such by David Sheppard in his book *Built as a City* and represents what is now a national, and even a universal phenomenon.

Within this turmoil the Christian Church has witnessed and worked at all the levels I have listed. Today, church buildings carry a wide variety of messages. Congregations gather for worship, evangelism takes place at many levels, social action responds to human needs, political relationships remain uneasy, the theme of personal morality still outweighs corporate concerns, the process of secularisation is accelerating and the cultural/class tensions still exist. Signs of hope can, over a long historical perspective, be seen in:

- The continuing strength of Roman Catholicism. Strategically placed churches, Catholic schools and the presence of three religious orders in West Ham assist in providing a constant and powerful framework.
- Protestant churches – in spite of retrenchment, introversion, lack of professional ministry, and theo-

logical uncertainty – still contain lively, strongly rooted fellowships.
- New congregations are constantly emerging. The growth of at least thirty black Churches has been paralleled by the arrival of house churches. All are biblically rooted and evangelical in ethos.
- Changes in attitudes within churches as team and group ministries operate, experiments in worship and research into programmes take place and a willingness to welcome and accept spiritual trends is evident.
- Indigenous commitment is growing as young couples decide to stay and the "believer-drain" is easing! By the use of housing associations, residential accommodation and active encouragement churches are retaining key personnel.
- Theological differences have given way to a mutual acceptance and appreciation.
- Wider concern as national groups and committed communities begin to face the problems and opportunities of what is now a major mission field.

The possibility of urban renewal has been explored by a wide variety of agencies in recent years and the churches have reflected both the repercussions of decline and the experiments in urban renewal. Patterns of Church life, organisational structures, traditional emphases and inner attitudes have all been affected. Urban mission takes place within this setting.

I am deeply grateful to West Ham. The place and the people have taught me so much. There is a realism and directness which is refreshing and there is a sense of history in the economic, racial and social struggles taking place there which echo the experience of so many of the world's population. Here I have found energetic and encouraging Christians facing and grappling with urban problems and seeking to carve out an authentic Christian presence in both the established and new forms of the Church of Christ.

If it is necessary to look closely at the roots of the social situation it is just as important for Christians to know where they have been in the past, to see where they are in the present, and to move into the future with a combination of understanding and hope. We are called to "make the Word flesh".

5

SIGNS OF STRESS

If you listen to the city you will hear the stress signals. They are insistent, disturbing and penetrating. Deep-rooted, widespread and growing in intensity – they are the cries of the urban.

Dramatised in the riots, visualised in the documentaries and analysed in the surveys these stress signals stream out. They are savagely and bluntly summarised in the visible graffiti:

Stop evicting Squatters   Kill Wogs
Jobs not Jails   Fight Unemployment
Jesus Saves, He's lucky   Stamp out Rent Act
Department of Stealth & Total
  Obscurity   Help!
Bring back the neighbourhood What about *me*?
Retire at 16, Vote at 18   Pakis stink

This is writing on the wall at another level: these signs are urgent warnings for the future. The messages are clear: we know deprivation. We face poverty. We experience division. We feel powerless. We are confused.

DEPRIVATION

Deprivation is an unpleasant word for an ugly reality. It has to do with a taking away. It is a denial, a removal, a withdrawal and a withholding. This deprivation is known in unemployment, poor housing, a drab environment and a general lack of choice. It leads to disadvantage and distress and ends in hardship and want. Urban deprivation is a cluster of factors. It is the clear and inevitable consequence of those social and economic forces which bear down on the people.

These forces remove the factories that provide the jobs, so unemployment levels in a place like Liverpool are twice the national average. Without a good income, cars become an impossibility so the figure of households without a car is double in the metropolitan areas.

Deprivation is accentuated by the continuing outward movement of population which often draws away the economically active people. Population in the central areas of Manchester, Liverpool, Birmingham and Newcastle declined by more than 20% during the decade 1971-81.

Deprivation is seen and known daily through the impact of the media. The visual comparison between the envied and unattainable style of living of the I.T.V. advertisements and the known realities is a constant reminder of the gulf between the "haves" and the "have nots".

Deprivation is acknowledged by the variety of Government responses within the Urban Programme. Educational Priority Areas tackled inequalities in school standards and achievements. The Urban Aid Programmes provided financial resources to rectify the imbalances of the inner city. Housing Action Areas concentrated on the inadequacy of homes – in numbers and quality. Community Development Projects revealed the lack of resources in neighbourhoods and the lack of co-ordination in local authority services. The Inner City Programme was explicitly concerned with economics and environment as well as the alleviation of social problems.

Urban deprivation is a condition of life that saps initiative and creates despair. When Sir Keith Joseph used the term "cycle of deprivation" in 1972 he set out to explain the persistence of inequality through the argument that deprivation is transmitted through the family. It is, of course, true that some lines of inadequacy do run through the generations but this ignores the economic causes of deprivation and deflects attention from the need to redistribute resources.

The Inner Cities Directorate of the Department of the Environment published their own notes on the 1981 Census Information and provided some startling insights into the contemporary political and economic map. A Ministry league table of urban deprivation showed the deprivation scores of ten London Boroughs to be worse than anything found in districts outside the capital. All are areas of "multiple deprivation" which have fallen into a cycle of decline because of the combination of problems such as high unemployment, overcrowded housing, high numbers of single parents or pensioners living alone, and a big exodus of population.

The statisticians started with eight indicators of deprivation for which figures were available. These were percentages in each local authority area for unemployment, overcrowded households, single parent households, households lacking exclusive use of basic amenities, population change, mortality rate and households whose head was born in the New Commonwealth or Pakistan.

The very first Urban Programme Circular, sent out in October 1968, said:

> The government proposed to initiate an urban programme of expenditure mainly on education, housing, health and welfare in areas of special social need. These were localised districts which bear the marks of multiple deprivation, which may show itself, for example, by way of notable deficiencies in the physical environment, particularly housing; overcrowding of houses; family sizes above the average; persistent unemployment; a high proportion of children in trouble or in need of care; or a combination of these. A substantial degree of immigrant settlement would also be an important factor, though not the only factor, in determining the existence of special social need.

Seventeen years on, the situation has changed. Deprivation is worse, not better; more widespread, less localised; evident not hidden; reaching more sections of the community, not fewer.

POVERTY

Behind the statistics of urban deprivation are the people who make up the urban poor. In *Poverty in the U.K.*[1] by Peter Townsend, the survey concludes that five million (9%) of the population were living beneath the state poverty line and fourteen million (26%) were living in "relative poverty". But the figures are for 1968! Since then the lines have deepened, the process has accelerated and the urban poor have grown both in numbers and area.

The Third World knows absolute poverty. We know relative poverty. But the causes are the same – economic forces bearing down upon the lives of people. And the consequences are clear. A Methodist minister in Belfast wrote:

> Those who inhabit the slums and twilight zones of Belfast are the less adequate who, because of their inability to cope, become more and more deprived. They have the less well rewarded jobs – if they have jobs at all. They see life in terms of immediate gratification and lack long-term goals. Not knowing how to budget their wages or their social welfare benefit, they spend unwisely and so their living conditions deteriorate. Those who have any will or spirit left may break out of the scene. The wounds are clearly visible. That some are self-inflicted does not make the festering any less easy to behold or the pain any less real. Thus the more deprived and "beat-up" a community becomes the more it deteriorates and the harder it is to bring new life.[2]

The urban poor are to be defined by comparison. If income is so much lower than the rest of society that a home cannot afford the kind of goods and conditions accepted as essential by other homes, then a line has been drawn and each side knows where it stands.

Poverty prevents participation in the life of the community and creates deprivation of a moral as well as a material type. This leads to the creation of an underclass – a term for those who are denied full participation or citizenship in their societies. It refers to employed workers who do the least desirable jobs but are often denied the basic legal, political and social rights of the rest of the labour force. Alternatively, it may refer to particular groups whose poverty derives from their non-employment; the long-term unemployed, single parent families, the elderly. Such long-term poverty prevents people from sharing the full life of a basically affluent community.

The creation of the urban poor in the UK has come about through a variety of factors:

- The *Creaming-Off* process by which the exodus of the young and the able has been encouraged by public policies related to taxation (mortgages) and transportation (commuters) producing demographic and economic decline.
- The *Sifting-Out* process by which jobs and skilled workers have become suburbanised, leaving the unskilled trapped and unemployed in the inner areas.
- The *Breakdown* of solidarity in the traditional working class structures, whether in the family kinship groups or the political trade unions.
- The *Social Detachment* of incoming professionals who do not share the realities of poverty, have a high turnover rate, cannot fully understand the ethos of and do not intend to settle among the urban poor.
- The *Addition of the Vulnerable* seeking anonymity, work, or refuge. The inner cities have more than their fair share of vagrants and addicts.
- The *Infusion of Immigrants*. The Caribbean people coming to do manual work, and the Asians living near each other for security, have replaced the outward-bound white population.

- The *Acceleration of Feelings*: – the increasing sense of
  impermanence and insecurity matches the visible and
  experienced evidence of a "running down".
- The *Hiddenness of the Situation*: – if you do not see
  the inner city you do not know what is going on. If you
  do not know what is going on you cannot be expected to
  take any action.

It is hard to number the urban poor. At the most extreme
level we do not know how many individuals live in near
destitution on the streets of our cities. By their very nature
they are outside the normal counting mechanisms of
society. The Campaign for the Homeless and Rootless
(C.H.A.R.) estimated in 1980 that there were as many as
100,000 persons in Great Britain without permanent
shelter, sometimes living in public or voluntary hostels
and overnight shelters and sometimes sleeping out. Not
enough is known about their daily lives or their income
but workers in this field describe them as the poorest of the
poor. Most of these are to be found living in, but not
accepted by, the inner city.

The measure used by the Policy Studies Institute, (the
long-term rate of Supplementary Benefit adjusted to
reflect more adequately the cost of children) produces a
figure of 6.1 million individuals living in three million
households who were in poverty in 1975. This represented
14.8% of all households and 11.3% of persons in the
population. This figure is now much higher, chiefly
because of the effects of long-term unemployment and of
wage rises below the rate in inflation for low-paid
workers.

Another official measure (for 1977) counts those within
a wider poverty band. Counting those with incomes below
Supplementary Benefit level, those on benefit, and those
with income 10%, 20% and 40% above the Supplementary Benefit level, the grand total is fourteen million
individuals in 7.6 million families, or 25% of the
population.

Townsend's survey of poverty in the U.K. using the

same poverty band yielded rather higher figures – 17.6 million individuals – and he suggested that this was a more accurate count than the official figures because the samples used by the latter tend to be under-representative of the poor.

As the figures above have shown, the goal of eradicating poverty has not been achieved. Indeed, the numbers with incomes below that required for basic needs are increasing, not declining. However one juggles the figures or argues with the categories there is a disturbingly high percentage trapped below the poverty line in a still affluent nation – and this is only the financial aspect.

The titles and dates of the books on my bookshelves indicate the progression of concern and response: *The Poor and the Poorest* (1965), *Poverty in the United Kingdom* (1979), *Inner City Poverty in Paris and London* (1981), *The Politics of Poverty* (1982), *Government and Urban Policy* (1983), *The Scandal of Poverty* (1983), *Poor Britain* (1985). Further, present Government policies make little attempt to divert any of the benefits of economic growth towards tackling poverty, whether that be in the depressed U.K. regions, inner cities or general housing conditions. In fact, many of the cuts envisaged in the Government's Expenditure Plans will make matters worse. No doubt this scale of priorities does reflect the desire of some for tax-cutting. But tax-cutting for some can mean life-line cutting for others.

DIVISION

We have two nations on one island. The idea is not new, observers, politicians, and Church leaders were all referring to the dimension a century ago. Novelists and sociologists wrote about the continuing divisions in the 1930s and 1950s. More recently demonstrations, pressure groups, national newspapers and T.V. have all underlined the reality of the two nations. What is new, and profoundly disturbing, is that divisions are widening and deepening, and misunderstanding and hostility characterise both sides.

Obervers noted the gap between two ways of life early in
the nineteenth century. Writing in 1832 under the title
*The Moral and Physical conditions of the Working
Classes employed in the Cotton Manufacture in Manchester* a social observer commented:

> That the evils of poverty and pestilence among the
> working classes of the close alleys, the crowded courts,
> the overpeopled habitations of wretchedness, where
> pauperism and disease congregate round the sources of
> social discontent and political disorder in the centre of
> our large towns – that these evils should have been
> overlooked by the aristocracy of country, cannot excite
> surprise. Very few of their order reside in, or near our
> large provincial towns.

Politicians commented. Benjamin Disraeli the Conservative Prime Minister said in 1880: "I was told that the
privileged and the people formed two nations."[3]

Church leaders confirmed. Canon Barnett, pioneer of
the Settlement movement, wrote in 1895: "The two
nations, that of the rich and that of the poor, are very
evident. Each grows strong, and the danger of collision is
the great danger of our time."

Novelists discovered. J.B. Priestly, at the height of the
economic depression in 1933, was collecting material for
his book *English Journey* and told of the discovery of three
Englands – the old England of the guide-books, nine-
teenth-century industrial England, and the twentieth-
century England of by-passes and suburbia.

Sociologists analysed. In a trend report on Urban
Sociology in 1955, Ruth Glass looked back: "In the towns
– certainly until the first world war – Britain's class
structure was reduced to a frightening simplicity; here
Disraeli's two nations met and then turned their backs
upon one another; here wealth was manufactured and
poverty accumulated. The cities were 'the crowded
nurseries of disease' and 'the devil's hot-beds of evil and
crime'."[4]

Denominations have responded. In 1981 the Methodists

launched a "Two Nations – One Gospel" campaign with five aims:

- To expose the divisions of society today.
- To arouse the Christian conscience about poverty and deprivation.
- To study the Gospel as good news for the poor.
- To support places and activities which represent Christ's mission among the poor.
- To motivate the whole Church to share in the Church's mission among the needy in the cities.

Pressure groups emphasised. Just before the General Election of 1983 the Chairman of a new crusading group, Church Action on Poverty, wrote to all the political parties: "What is needed as soon as the new Parliament is elected is immediate help for the poor and to stop the disintegration of our society into two nations. We are still a comparatively wealthy country. We ask you to help that wealth to help the worse off."

Newspapers accepted. A *Guardian* editorial in August 1983 referred to the book by Paul Harrison on Hackney, the T.V. programme *Breadline Britain* and a speech by the Labour politician, Roy Hattersley: "We live... in a profoundly unequal society. We are not so much two nations – a concept to which even the wetter end of the Conservative party still make occasional obeisance – but four or five. Progress has cut mortality rates everywhere; yet it still remains the case that the mortality rates for mothers in the lowest social class are twice those for mothers in the highest."

Television has portrayed. Whether that be in the documentaries like *Am I my Brother's Keeper?* or *Divided Britain* or intellectually in programmes like the Dimbleby Lecture of 1984 in which David Sheppard, the Bishop of Liverpool, referred to "Comfortable Britain" and the "Other Britain": "There really are two Britains. There is what I call Comfortable Britain. I imagine that most of you see yourselves, as I do, as part of comfortable, fairly successful, middle Britain. I make no apology for attempting tonight to persuade you to stand in the shoes of the Other Britain, of whom I see a great deal.''

The long-standing historical divisions within our society have not been removed by the Welfare State. The underlying, hidden divisions have been exacerbated and sharpened by recession and political policy. We are two nations *financially*. A study, *Unequal Fringes*, by the Low Pay Unit in February 1984 claimed that the rapid growth of perks has divided the employed into the haves and the have-nots, a situation which is not only unfair but also creates great resentment. A company director earning a basic salary of £25,000 a year can have fringe benefits worth an extra £12,500 through lengthy paid holidays, pensions, company cars, medical insurance and even subsidised housing. The low-paid, whose perks may begin and end in the company canteen, lose out in every way. They even contribute to the cost of all perks through an increasing tax burden.

We are two nations *politically*. A political map of constituencies in the U.K. in 1984 shows all the Labour seats clustered within the major conurbations centred on the vast new housing estates or based on the areas of traditional industry. In London the inner ring of boroughs alongside the Thames form a solid, encircled Labour enclave within the spreading, suburban ring of Conservative seats.

We are two nations *educationally*. A glance at the ladder of educational authorities sending school leavers on to further education indicates clearly that Shire and Sub-urban authorities are at the top and inner city authorities at the bottom.

We are two nations *socially*. Attitudes polarise. A list of accepted differences spells out the viewpoints and life-styles of two different worlds:

Owner-occupier	Rented from council or private landlord
Car owner	Public transport

Monthly salary	Weekly wage-packet
Perks	Basic wage
Further education	Leave school at sixteen
Professional, Managerial	Manual worker
Churchgoing	Non-churchgoing
White population	Cosmopolitan
Gardens	Tower blocks
Guardian/Daily Telegraph/The Times	*Sun/Daily Mirror*

Attitudes to poverty are more sharply divided in this country than in any other in Europe. The belief that poverty is self-inflicted, due to personal inadequacy or the consequence of laziness is deeply held. The view that people deliberately make themselves homeless, cheerfully engage in the black economy, or light-heartedly enter prostitution is only true of a very tiny minority of our society. The great majority of the urban poor desperately search for work, struggle to attain decent housing, have strong moral standards but are continually pressured by lack of opportunity, skill or resource within a society which appears to operate on the basis of "To those who have it shall be given. From those who have not it shall be taken away." Those – and I am among that number – who look on from relative security and different life-styles need to know the circumstances and see the power of hidden forces that bear down on the lives of so many people before we make quick and flip judgements.

POWERLESS

The realities of power and powerlessness are not exclusive to the inner city or the council estate but there they are sharply focussed and experienced. On a major scale they surface in the world of planning, illustrated in the future of the London Docklands. Recession, containerisation and shifting transport patterns have turned great areas of East and South London into an industrial ghost area.

Initially, those London boroughs facing the decline and the future of the docks grouped together in a joint planning exercise that involved widespread public participation. But now the imposition by Parliament of the London Docklands Development Corporation has removed consultation and accountability and a distant, politically inspired body presides over the usage and control of the land. Local people feel locked out and powerless.

On a more personal scale the inability to operate the "switchboard" of information networks leads to widespread frustration. Communication skills, articulateness, availability of knowledge, access to influence and other "know-how" are often lacking. Apathy, impotent rage, futile violence, or lack of self-confidence follows.

One of my first hurtful pastoral experiences in East London was to learn that I (then wearing a dog-collar!) could discover that a boy had leukaemia from hospital staff when the parents had been unable to secure such information! During the time the local Citizen's Advice Bureau was at Lawrence Hall I saw a daily flood (totalling 9,000 a year) of local people unable to cope with the complexities of our society. The advice, and often advocacy, of trained professionals and volunteers was one attempt to redress powerlessness.

We all sit uncomfortably with power. Few will admit to having it, fewer still to wanting it! But the possession and exercise of power in our society is granted to one section and removed from another.

Christians in the U.K. are concerned about power and powerlessness. In 1974 David Sheppard, then Bishop of Woolwich and now Bishop of Liverpool wrote *Built as a City* with a section dealing with the experience of powerlessness at the levels of work (who makes the decisions?), race (to be black is to be disadvantaged) and community (who controls the resources?).

In 1979 the radical One for Christian Renewal Movement held a triennial Conference on Power and drew on a paper by Andrew Morton, then Secretary of the

British Council of Churches which was part of the British Today and Tomorrow Programme. This paper, and the conference, was concerned with the nature and types of power, the location and abuse of power, the character and incidence of powerlessness. It tackled power within the Churches and moved towards a theology of power.

In 1980 the Inner City Group of the Shaftesbury Project produced, from the evangelical wing, *Powerlessness and the Inner City*, which used modern examples and scripture to earth the debate. Beginning with the actual experience of the inner city the booklet moved from the current distribution of power towards a theology of the city.

Three conclusions were drawn by all the writers and thinkers:

- Power is *unequally distributed* to the continuing disadvantage of certain sections of our societies, especially those known as the urban poor.
- Our society has a basic *conflict of interests* which lies behind the symptoms of power and powerlessness.
- The causes of the problems are in the *wider economic and social processes* of our society within which the inner city and the commuter suburbs are two manifestations of one set of processes.

It is true that we have tried to redistribute power through positive discrimination, agency co-ordination and public participation but these are superficial. The sharpness of the problem is mitigated but not eradicated. The proferred solutions are a poultice, not radical surgery.

Robert Holman, in his book *Poverty: Explanations of Social Deprivation*, summarises the position:

Britain consists of a stratified society within which resources in terms of income, wealth and power, are unequally divided. Poverty functions to service and justify these divisions. The existence of the poor, who are held to be responsible for their poverty, implies that the position of the more affluent should be left unchallenged. In addition, the socially deprived provide a society with a pool of workers who have no choice but to take the state's most unattractive occupations. Further, they are so powerless that they cannot oppose being used as the "regulators" by which the economic system can be controlled.

Power still resides overwhelmingly with the educated middle class. They have contacts, access to lawyers and accountants, the capacity to articulate and publicise their views, the ability to organise, and our educational system assumes that their culture is the norm.

In the final analysis, power ends in politics. The decision-makers who allocate resources, determine life-styles, and regulate the financial system are in the world of politics. And it is here that Christians find themselves in an uncomfortable dis-eased position. A course I chaired in 1983 in London on "Power and Powerlessness in the City" ended with a group of young Christians expressing their need for information and understanding about the political world – this, they considered, was their area of greatest ignorance.

It has also become the arena of confusion and bitterness. The struggles between metropolitan boroughs and central Government; the tensions between the new left and the traditional socialists, the polarisation of employers and trade unions, the violence engendered by extreme right-wing groups and, above all, the apparent impotence of party politics all combine to make people back away.

CONFUSED

Religion is now on the side-lines of life and the closure of many inner city church buildings and the marginalisation of the clergy are but two obvious symptoms of a deeper malaise.

Within the thought-world of the individual we have lost the dominance of religious motive and symbolism, and religion itself has become a purely personal concern. Modern stress on the scientific and the observable has pushed out the mysterious. There is a rejection of the reverential, loss of awe, a decrease in depth, a withering of dedication balanced by an increase in cynicism and indifference.

The Christian Faith is not on its own in struggling with the corrosive acids of the secular age. Secularisation is a universal phenomenon and is just as acute for the Muslim and Hindu working to sustain a religious fabric within the inner city as for the Christian holding a long-established faith.

The confusion of inner attitudes is expressed in a reaction towards cults, mysticism, astrology and superstition. The expulsion of one belief is inevitably followed by the vacuum-filling arrival of another philosophy. Pluralisation compounds the problem as a selection of competing world-views visibly thrust themselves upon the people of the inner city – mosques and temples now stand alongside churches and synagogues. Everything is now open to question, especially those areas of life which traditionally have been accepted in an uncritical way – the family, marriage, life-style and faith. This uncertainty has actively encouraged the privatisation of religion, the lifting of religion out of the every-day realities.

While it is of course true that all of society is increasingly secularised there is an intensity about secularisation in the inner city. The social balancing of an intellectual culture and the counterpoint of the rural are both absent and there is an immediacy and pressure which works away beneath the surface, deep within the minds of men and women. Secular values have affected the Church, obscured her mission, and have eroded her credibility in the world.

These signs taken together make up a message. Deprivation... poverty... division... powerlessness... confusion, all spell out the themes of inequality and injustice.

In one year, 1980, Christians of the world recognised the universal emergence of the urban poor in the ecumenical World Council of Churches Conference in Melbourne,

Australia; the evangelical Consultation on World Evangelisation in Pattaya, Thailand; and the Roman Catholic
debate in Latin America over the pastoral and political
role of the Church. The changing terminology carried the
shift in understanding. This has spilt over to Britain.
Christian concern has moved from the inner city (the
place) through urban mission (the programme) to the
urban poor (the people). We are now wrestling with the
word priority – already used in the national Urban
Priority Areas and now taken up by the Archbishop of
Canterbury's Commission on Urban Priority Areas.

Anticipating the conclusions of that commission the
Archbishop of Canterbury stirred controversy at a service
in St. Paul's Cathedral in March 1985 when he referred to
the inner cities: "We don't have to look as far as Ethiopia
to find the darkness of disease, death and disaster. It is here
on our doorsteps." At a later Press conference he was asked
to define "darkness". He replied: "A sense of life having
little meaning, that your aspirations are frustrated and
your human relationships damaged and that you cannot
succeed. That sort of feeling creates the darkness into
which we want to bring light."

6

STIRRINGS AND SHAKINGS

The subterranean rumblings of the 1930s and the volcanic eruptions of the 1939–45 war set shock waves coursing into the whole of British Society – including the Churches. The social stirrings that followed led to a period of searching and the emergence of new responses. The agitation moved on to shake some of the fundamental bastions of Church life, especially in the inner cities. The pressures came from many directions in bewildering and unexpected fashions. Few could have expected wealth-creating areas like Merseyside and the London Docklands to swing so rapidly into dependence and deprivation. Fewer still could have forecast the waves of immigration that would alter the face and attitudes of the inner city.

Within my own life-time I have journeyed from the established, and apparently endurable suburban Church that was building-based and minister-centred into a turmoil of congregations, projects and networks. The process has been painful for me – and for many others. The heritage we valued has been called into question, the viewpoints we held have been challenged and the life-style we planned has radically altered.

Many factors and forces have joined together to create such an alteration, and it is these I shall be looking at in this chapter.

INDUSTRIAL MISSION

The toughness and realism of the industrial world in Britain was the setting for some germinal initiatives. The

largely Anglican Sheffield Industrial Mission began as the
war was ending (1944) and the leader, Ted Wickham,
produced a book, *Church and People in an Industrial
City*[1], that documented in detail the weakness of the
Church in Sheffield. The inter-denominational South
London Industrial Mission (S.L.I.M.) followed in 1948
and the Methodist-inspired Luton Industrial Mission was
opened in 1954 led by Bill Gowland. The Scottish
counterpart was the Iona Community, founded by George
McLeod, that drew together workers from the urban/
industrial centres of Scotland.

The influence of these pioneers was to spread to such a
degree that by 1978 nearly 400 industrial chaplains –
sometimes in teams 20–30 strong – were operating in all
the major industrial centres of the U.K. But there were
serious implications of having priests in secular settings.
The adequacy of the traditional pastoral and parochial
ministry was questioned, the middle class domination of
the Church was exposed, the evangelistic task was seen to
be massive and the political involvements were radically
unsettling.

Overseas, parallel industrial missions ran into trouble.
First in France, the arena of the Roman Catholic worker-
priests; and then in the U.S.A., the scene of large and
powerful industrial missions, the Church terminated the
projects. Authority was withdrawn, funding dried up, and
approval disappeared. *Requiem for American Industrial
Missions* written in 1974, summed up the decline:

> But as the civil rights movement faded and public
> concern for the urban crisis abated, money for this kind
> of programme became increasingly hard to secure. By
> 1970 the Church's interest in most such social issues
> seemed on the wane. And when the Church's prosperity
> declined ... most easily cut from the hard pressed
> church budgets were projects like industrial missions
> which brought in neither converts or funds.[2]

In Britain patterns and pressures were different. Although
industrial man was unchurched and increasingly secular-

ised there was not the ideological opposition to the Church France knew. Neither did the British Churches lose the belief that the laity was the proper presence of the Church in the world. Yet the experience, questions and projects that surfaced from industrial missions in the U.K. shook the Church and inspired individuals and groups to face the wider scenario of working class culture.

PASTORAL EXPERIENCE

The shop-floor experience of industrial chaplains was confirmed by those who worked as pastors and priests in the housing areas. The 1945 Anglican report entitled *Towards the Conversion of England* argued that national- ly about 15% of the people regularly attended a place of worship; probably about 30% went on some special occasion; some 40–50 % were quite indifferent to religion; and the remaining 10% were hostile. But national figures of church attendance have always been at least three times those for the industrial areas, and witnesses from a broad spectrum of churchmanship and areas were soon under- lining the reality of the gulf between the Church and the people.

From Glasgow in 1954 the Church of Scotland minister Tom Allan wrote vividly in *The Face of my Parish*[3] of the situation he met in the parish of North Kelvinside:

> At the very outset I was to realise that there was only the most tenuous bond between the parish and the parish church. In a parish of ten thousand souls, in 1946 the communicant membership of North Kelvinside stood at just over four hundred; and of that number perhaps a quarter lived within the actual bounds of the parish itself. Out of nearly two thousand homes less than a hundred claimed a connection with their parish church.

As Tom Allan led his congregation into a sustained visitation campaign other leaders stressed different answers. In Leeds the Anglican Ernie Southcott sought to bridge the gap between the Church and the people with an extensive network of house groups. In Coventry the new cathedral initiated special courses for the clergy after the 1968 People and Cities Conference. In Sheffield the Methodist John Vincent linked small churches, developed cell groups, and urged theological reflection, and his conclusion was summed up in *Starting All Over Again*[4].

The starting point was always the same. The gulf, the gap and the separation. The methods were bridges, an attempt to span the divide. Whether it was door knocking, house groups in every street, changed clerical attitudes, local leadership or new experiments – the motive was missionary, the methods were pragmatic. Pastoral experience stood four-square with industrial chaplaincy in emphasising that the Word had not been made flesh for huge sections of the British population. The message coming through was clear – great areas of Britain were mission fields, traditional methods had failed, pioneering and experimenting initiatives were forging new models.

FRONTIER GROUPS

New literature like *The New Christian* and the *Auden-shaw Papers* came into being as a result of this post-war world of stirring and agitation. Among the literature the correspondence journal *Christians in Industrial Areas* set out its own aim:

The mission field today is the urban scene. It may be inner city, overspill estates around the city, or in the new towns. It is here that the Church is weakest and most vulnerable. "Christians in Industrial Areas" is a correspondence for those interested in, or working in these areas, to hear, share and explore our failures and successes, ideas and problems. We try to look at the urban scene as Christians and come to a deeper understanding of it, sharing in its pain and joy, frustrations and opportunities, and seek to understand the Gospel in this culture. We try to look at the wider developments within the Church and try and evaluate them in terms of the urban scene.

In the Midlands the William Temple College (then in Rugby) wrestled with social questions and the Church's contribution. In London the Notting Hill Ecumenical Centre, placed at the site of the first British race riots of 1958, sought to help Christians understand the city:

> The Ecumenical Centre Workshop on Urban Ministry for Theological Students is conceived to help prepare them for a radically new way of ministry within urban society. Its aim is to give the theological students a unique awareness of the city, to develop a relevant theological perspective and to equip them with a method by which the Gospel can effectively engage the city's life on all levels.

By action and experiment, through gifted individuals and committed groups, combining projects and reflections, a series of Frontier Groups joined the experience of industrial mission and pastoral experience to expose the situation and to sketch some ways to cross the frontiers.

INTERNATIONAL INFLUENCES

The shakings and stirrings known in Britain were influenced by, and often coincided with, movements in other countries. In France the priest-worker movement led by Abbe Godin and written up in *France Pagan* (1949)[5] by Maisie Ward sought, but failed, to shift the focus of action from the parish system to the industrial mission field. The Lay Academies of Germany drew together Christians for training and support. From the U.S.A. *Come out the Wilderness* (1962)[6], an account by an Englishman, Bruce Kenrick, of a Protestant parish in New York, *Secular City* (1965)[7], a celebration of the urban by Harvey Cox, and the *Suburban Captivity of the Churches* (1962)[8] by Gibson Winter (an analysis of Protestant responsibility in the expanding metropolis) stood alongside a flurry of Urban Training Centres in cities like Detroit, Chicago and Boston. European experiment and American analysis coincided with U.K. concern and stimulated a major British conference in Cambridge in 1969 on the diverse urban programmes and responses emerging in the U.K.

The World Council of Churches Conference on Church and Society in 1966 summarised the problem for the European and North American Churches:

> The problem of the contemporary structure of the Church is that it was devised for a past form of society, which was static, generally agrarian, and religiously conformist. Essentially the same structure was exported in the era of missionary expansion...
> It is, however, a fact that today this form of society is becoming increasingly atypical, as urbanisation and industrialisation become characteristic of all societies...
> The logic of this situation requires that the Church be expressed in terms of mission in its biblical range of prophecy, proclamation and obedient service in the world.

Urban Training Centres became the model, providing the focus and the impetus. *Urban*: this was now seen to be the zone which was determining patterns of life, creating massive human problems, and the place of weakness for the Church. *Training*: acknowledging that equipping for mission was needed by all (whether lay or clerical), that new tasks required new forms, that action and reflection were both essential and that biblical insight had to be married to contemporary programmes. *Centres*: in order to localise and root, gather and unify, providing a comprehensive overview, offering a springboard and support for action.

SHAKINGS

These stirrings, whether socially or spiritually orientated, reached right into the most visible manifestations of Church life in Britain – buildings, membership and ministry. For generations the church as the place, membership as the people, and the clergy/minister as the central person coalesced to present the Church and the Gospel as understood in British eyes. Within the inner cities of the U.K. these three pillars were to shake. At first the negative aspects of questioning the place of building, noting the decline in membership and experiencing the uncertainty of the ministerial role misted over the emerging excitement and opportunities of renewal, fresh approaches, and a return to biblical roots.

...IN BUILDINGS

Post-war redevelopment and renewal on a massive scale either physically removed traditional local churches or else exposed them to a sea of new, contrasting buildings. The depletion of the population led to redundant churches and mergers and Church authorities looked for other usages for the unwanted buildings. Maintenance budgets soared as heating and labour costs accelerated for huge buildings with dwindling congregations.

The first level of response ran along three lines:

Adaptation took place as areas were screened off for smaller congregations and community pressures for wider usage pressed Church authorities into a fresh understanding of the stewardship of resources but also precipitated uncomfortable divisions between those who saw the church buildings as a legacy for themselves and those who wanted to open the doors to all. Multi-purpose buildings, whether newly planned or adapted, became the order of the day.

The second level of response finds illustration in the results of a survey in Bradford, Derby and Lambeth, three multi-racial and multi-faith areas, summed up in the B.C.C. report *Church Property and People* (1973) by Ann Holmes. This was a study of the *attitudes* of Churches to their property. Considerable differences of view exist about the significance of the sanctuary, theologically and psychologically. The financial burden of buildings dominates and diverts attention, and much time and energy have to be channelled into raising money for fabric funds – and in the maintenance and management. In a subtle way, the inherited array of buildings may over-influence or even determine the activities and involvement of the church group concerned, especially in its relation-ship to the non-churchgoing people of the area. Church-related manpower is forced into a role of youth-worker/caretaker/accountant. Questions about the centrality of buildings often begin from the financial and time demands but in the inner city they are intensified by the pressures from the community for use (what will happen to our buildings then?), by the request from other Christian groupings (should we really have a black church here?) and even more, the presence of non-Christian faiths (how can Hindus be allowed to use our halls?).

The third level of response is a much more *radical questioning* of buildings. The coming of house churches, cultural congregations and, above all, the growing stress on house groups or base Christian committees have all begun from the opposite end – referring more to the scriptural pattern of Acts 2: 42–47, the power of the group, and the naturalness of home-based cells. Whenever larger buildings are needed for larger congregational worship halls can be hired in schools or community centres.

The emerging pattern is not yet fully clear for all three forces are currently in play. Traditional congregations are physically adapting their buildings or extending their usage. The pressures of pluralism, whether it be multi-racial or multi-faith, are reshaping the programmes and the skylines of the inner city as mosques and temples stand alongside the homes of black churches. And the deeper, insistent notes of lifestyle, evangelism and fellowship stir congregations from beneath the surface.

The first question for Christians is not "What should we do with our buildings?", but "What is our role as the Church?" Then, and only then will we know what buildings (if any) we really need and how best to utilise them. Mission must come before maintenance.

The second question about buildings has to do with stewardship. That sense of accountability may appear to the congregation to be centred on the problems of finance and the heavy use of time but there are deeper questions which have to do with wider community usage and the sharing of buildings. Whenever Churches jealously keep their buildings for themselves they proclaim a message to their community. Whenever the new Churches are rebuffed and the possibility of sharing not considered, a practical expression of fellowship is broken.

The problem and paradox of church buildings in the inner city is highlighted in a West Ham Church Life Survey in 1984. Eight out of twenty-three Churches in the district where I live have emerged in the last fifteen years. These new, often growing Churches rarely have buildings of their own. As the report says: "It seems crazy that while about one third of the Churches find their buildings a burden, another third have no buildings of their own and are very keen to find one."[9]

MEMBERSHIP

The people who gather in the church buildings of the inner city are the barometer of faith, the spiritual Gallup poll. They reflect the stirrings and shakings, they carry within themselves the hurt and the healing of the city. Paradoxes abound: an overall, long drawn-out decline in numbers over against many dramatic, developing stories of growth; traditional, resistant, ageing congregations alongside flexible, young, vigorous new churches; fellowships grouped around a strong, authoritarian leader or open "body-ministry" churches where participation is active and authentic.

Behind the statistics are two clear conclusions: overall decline and changes in constituency. Long years of decline have gone on throughout most of this century – nationally, but especially among the urban poor. In the

1970s the British Churches lost 1,000,000 members, closed 1,000 churches and lost 2,500 ministers. But *Prospect for the Eighties* – a census of the churches in 1979 undertaken by the Nationwide Initiative in Evangelism – pointed out:

> The decline in church attendance in Inner London is the greatest in the country. All churches together are declining at the rate of -2.9%. The nearest is another metropolitan county, Tyne and Wear, at -2.6%. Greater Manchester is declining at -2.0% per annum, Merseyside at -1.8%, West Yorkshire at -1.7% and the West Midlands at -1.1%. These figures indicate quite clearly the desperate plight of inner city churches.
>
> The four biggest Protestant denominations are all declining in Inner London, the only part of the whole of England where this is happening. The Church of England is declining at -3.3% per annum, more than three times the national average, the Methodists at -1.5%, four times the national average, the Baptists at -1.3% against a national average of 1.3% and the U.R.C./Congregational at -6.2% per annum, three times the national figure.
>
> The Roman Catholic Church is also declining in Inner London at -5.0% per annum against a national figure of -2.0%. This decline is the largest in England.[10]

Changes in the constituency of congregations are to be seen in two directions, statistical and spiritual. Since 1900 the Roman Catholics, then a minority group, have overtaken both Anglican and Free Church membership. But in the last twenty years the most dramatic change has been in the number of people going to the new, independent, mainly black congregations. The table tells its own story:

INNER LONDON

	1975		1979		Change per Annum	
	Adult Member-ship (000s)	Adult Atten-dance (000s)	Adult Member-ship (000s)	Adult Atten-dance (000s)	Adult Member-ship (%)	Adult Atten-dance (%)
ALL Churches	427	223	392	198	-2.1	-2.9
ALL Protestant	129	114	122	110	-1.3	-1.1
Episcopal	57	52	53	46	-2.1	-3.3
Methodist	10	10	8	10	-4.1	-1.5
Baptist	9	9	7	9	-6.0	-1.3
U.R.C./Congregational	5	4	4	3	-6.0	-6.2
Independent	6	6	6	7	+2.9	+4.2
African/West Indian	13	16	13	17	+1.1	+2.6
Pentecostal/Holiness	2	6	3	6	+4.1	+3.7
Other	28	11	28	11	+0.6	0.0
Roman Catholic	278	106	250	86	-2.6	-5.0
Orthodox	20	2	20	2	-0.3	-3.4

From *Prospect for the Eighties* (vol. 2)

But other patterns beside statistical ones need to be noted among Christian people of the inner cities. There has been a deepening realism, often a return to biblical roots, and a wrestling with the claims of evangelism (we are in a mission field) and social transformation (what about the poor?). Freer worship and more participation has run through many of the Churches. Young people have arrived to join the indigenous people and these "in-comers" have brought new life to some congregations. The presence of people from the Third World, whether Asia, Africa, or the Caribbean, has sharpened under-standing of the need for simplicity in living, stewardship, and conservation.

LEADERSHIP

The shaking-up process particularly affected the professionals of the Church. Within the urban areas the
clergy, ministers and priests were in pastoral control, but
culturally divided from those they tried to serve. The
division was accentuated by the size of vicarages, the use of
private schools, speech difference, clerical clothing and
the generally accepted status of the clergy.

A Congregationalist, John Pellow, summarised the
position in his book about Stepney, *Concrete Village*:

> The Church, unwieldy and immobile, with its roots
> deep in mediaevalism, came on the scene too slowly and
> too late to be part of the formative process. When it
> came, it came not as a part of life, but as something
> tacked on to it. Its representatives were from far different
> situations, from different cultural backgrounds and, if
> it's not begging the question, from different class levels.
> They were not of the East End and the message they had
> to deliver was not of the East End.[11]

Men and women placed in this position had to face many
problems, their own personal life-style, the expectations
carried in themselves and their congregations, and the
apparent intractability of the inner city ministry. Individualism began to give way to team ministries;
economic and theological pressures forged tent ministries;
the comprehensive, jack-of-all-trades minister was joined
by specialists in youth or social work. The need of
preparation for inner city ministry led to induction
courses while others began to train in their own context.

The extent of the shaking-up process became plain for
me when the East London Church leaders of two London
boroughs asked for an induction course in 1985 for men
and women coming into leadership roles in the churches
of Newham and Tower Hamlets. The planning group
comprised men and women, black and white, lay and
ordained, those in pastoral charge and those in wider

ministry: a Methodist minister heading a community renewal programme, two black pastors (a man and a woman), a Roman Catholic priest, a Baptist minister bridging Church and community work, an Anglican deaconess, an elder from one of the new Christian fellowships and the U.R.C. training officer. Those who joined the course presented an equally tangled medley of roles: they included a Methodist woman minister and a locally born Baptist lay pastor; an Anglican priest with a parish and a black evangelist; a woman elder from one of the new Churches and a Roman Catholic priest working within a team, a former Baptist minister working in a U.R.C. church and as part of a Methodist team, and a trained theological student serving in a Methodist community centre.

Out of the stirrings and shakings have come the signs of hope which are to be seen in urban mission today. The pioneers have lived to see their work take root and grow. From the burdens of buildings, the decline in membership and the questions of leadership have sprung new insights and signs of hope.

7

SIGNS OF HOPE

SEEDS AND CLUSTERS

Throughout the 1960s and into the 1970s the stirring and shaking experienced at so many levels in the inner city began to move into another phase. Gifted individuals (seeds) and committed groups (clusters) shared in a drawing together, in a linking of hands by concerned people.

By 1966 groups concerned with urban mission were already meeting in Liverpool. After the first race riots in this country the Notting Hill Ecumenical Centre surfaced in 1968 to help Christians of all persuasions and disciplines to face the consequences of immigration. Cardiff was advertising courses on "Doing Theology in the Secular City" by 1969 and in the Coventry Programme the traditional doctrines of man, sin, and God had counterpoints in psychology, sociology and theology. The Urban Mission Project in London went one stage further in its "Plunge". This was a technique used to immerse professionals in the life-style of the city at street level. With little money and few resources individuals learnt how to survive for a week in the inner city.

In Britain, as elsewhere in the world, it was evident by the mid-sixties and was confirmed in the seventies, that a wide variety of new patterns of urban ministry were already in being. No one pattern predominated and the projects had developed from the initiatives of individuals or groups, without a clear overall policy from the Church.

There was, therefore, a high mortality rate and no guarantee of continuity.

Behind all these emerging clusters lay three factors:

- A response to the growing post-war awareness of the acute problems the Church faced in urban and industrialised societies. .
- An embodiment of this in "charismatic" personalities who carried in themselves the awareness and the action-response.
- A growing theological conviction that God was at work in this rapidly changing society and that Christians were called to discern His action and to co-operate with it.

From these clusters sprang new structures, greater flexibility, indigenous leadership, a wave of incomers, retraining of the clergy, stress on teams, analysis, and a continuing and uncomfortable questioning of the accepted.

GREEN SHOOTS

The clustering together of individuals and groups was to lead from the 1970s into a rapid spread of green shoots. From the barren stubble of the industrial areas sprouted wave after wave of living – initially fragile – green shoots symbolising new life and hope pointing towards an urban harvest. Many were to wither and die, but others have grown strong and matted together to build a tough, deeply-rooted Christian presence penetrating all levels of urban life.

One of the features of the green shoots is their anonymity. The Directory of Christian groups, communities and networks[1] has 384 entries without a single named individual. This is in marked contrast to the personality cult of so many congregations and projects. The *group* is the significant factor, people are caught up by something greater than the individual.

A double thrust lay behind these shoots. One was the response of Christians to obvious areas of human need. Another was the evangelistic task Christ had laid on his Church. In biblical terms this double thrust is summed up in the Nazareth manifesto of Luke 4: 18-19 taken up by Jesus and in the Resurrection mandate of Matthew 28. Wherever I have gone in the inner cities of England, the U.S.A., or Australia, these have been the Scriptural poles. Too often it has been an "either ... or"; either social justice or personal conversion. The great need has been to hold both together. The two streams will then flow into the key model of 1 Corinthians 12 – the Body of Christ uniting believers in a total ministry of directed love towards the world in its anguish and yearning.

SOCIAL TRANSFORMATION

Those taking Luke 4 seriously have seen the biblical concern for the poor and oppressed paralleled within the contemporary categories of the dispossessed and powerless people of the urban poor. They have, in the name of Christ, tilted their lances at visible enemies embodied in racism, housing and unemployment. In these, and many other fields, Christians were engaged in the Kingdom task of social transformation.

Take racism. The coming of the Caribbean immigrants to do our work in the fifties and sixties and the Asian people to start new lives in the sixties and seventies created urgent practical problems and a racist reaction. Christians against Racism and Fascism (C.A.R.A.F) grew out of the political environment of the late 1970s which saw racist and fascist movements given political respectability and legitimacy through the media and through gains in local elections. Formed in 1978, C.A.R.A.F. is a non-denominational Christian response to developments in British society to which the Churches themselves were not adequately responding. Operating through workshops, conferences and publicity, C.A.R.A.F. affirmed racial justice and repudiated the activities of racist and fascist movements. In north-east London a group called ZEBRA (a self-explanatory name) worked with black and white Christians who together wanted to make Britain a just, multi-racial society. More locally, BADGER (again, self-explanatory) rooted this concern into the London Borough of Newham.

Take housing. The coming of housing associations as the third arm of housing, working alongside the provisions of local authorities and private landlords, opened a door to a wide variety of initiatives. In my own experience green shoots thrust up in all directions. I live in a complex where one housing association has met the needs of older people in sheltered housing and given help to young couples who want to live in the inner city – already twenty young couples have stayed, then settled in East London to provide a network of activists. Just across the road from us the Baptist Men's Movement Housing Association has created a village of sheltered housing flats and single units for younger people. Near me, a Springboard Housing Association development unites Anglicans and Methodists in a wide variety of projects while the Shaftesbury Housing Association maintains its concern for the handicapped by means of its sheltered housing complex. Multiply this across the country, add to it the hostels for the unemployed, the centres for the homeless, and the refuges for the addicts, and evidence mounts that concern has been translated into bricks and mortar.

Put alongside race and housing an almost endless catalogue of projects and schemes reaching out to answer the needs of the unemployed, the elderly, the inarticulate, the poverty-stricken and the broken families. Add to this the stress on community development, political involvement, and law and order concerns.

Put it all together and there is an astonishingly diverse and creative use of resources and gifts ready to match unmet human needs. But this is only one side of the signs of hope. Alongside the socially concerned groups is the wave of new churches.

NEW CHURCHES

It is impossible to keep up with the wealth of new churches that have become such a feature in the inner cities. Their numbers are phenomenal – there are at least 400 in London alone.

I have experienced this growth at first hand. Five congregations have begun life in Lawrence Hall, the centre where I work. The black-led Church of God Prophecy began with a handful of people in 1974 and subsequently moved on to a local church hall. The Seventh Day Adventists began a branch church in 1978 which has steadily grown into a strong, entirely black congregation. They were followed in 1982 by the Plaistow Christian Fellowship, a multi-racial offshoot congregation from In-Contact ministries. Then came the International Christian Centre, a largely Malaysian congregation breaking away from the local Assemblies of God Church. Finally, the Apostolic Church settled with us in 1983 and is almost entirely black in membership. All have a freedom and informality in worship, are evangelistic, Bible centred, close-knit fellowships. They vary in leadership styles through elders to pastors.

Overall, the new churches of the inner city fall into three broad categories – the cultural churches (mainly black, but including a wide variety of Afro-Caribbean, Asian and even European congregations); the community or fellowship churches (stemming from the charismatic movement but with a pronounced emphasis on the fellowship and life-style) and the planted churches (deliberately planned by denominations, rising from the embers of a dead congregation, or initiated by one of the para-church organisations).

CULTURAL CHURCHES

To some degree the cultural churches have always been with us. At the heart of our cities Welsh congregations and Scottish kirks can be found alongside churches built for

the expatriates of Europe. But the growth and proliferation of the black churches is a phenomenon in its
own right. The expansion has been rapid – seventy-seven
congregations were known in 1962, over 100 in 1963 and
390 by 1966. In 1977 there were 650 places of "black"
worship in multi-racial areas, with many hundreds of
other congregations hiring halls and churches. Roswith
Gerloff, in *Partnership in Black and White* reported that
these congregations belong to about 100–110 organisations, and that:

> Doctrinally, they belong to seven main denominational
> streams – Holiness, Pentecostal Trinitarian, Pente-
> costal Oneness, Adventist (Sabbatarian), African In-
> dependent (Aladura), Revivalistic (Latter Rain) move-
> ments and the Ethiopian Orthodox Church. Culturally,
> they reflect West African, East African, West Indian,
> North American White, North American Black and
> British influences. Some of them comprise up to 5,000
> members in more than 90 single congregations, some
> not more than 20 in a single group.[2]

There are five reasons for this new Christian presence
among the urban poor of the U.K.:

Immigration brought more than half a million West
Indians in the fifties and sixties into Britain. Most settled
in the inner cities into a physically bleak environment.
The Churchgoing background of the West Indian people
(one survey showed 69 % attending mainstream denominations in the Caribbean) contrasted with the low
percentage of neighbouring white working class people in
the settlement areas.
White rejection. West Indians reacted to both style
(formal, "cold" worship) and attitudes (at best they were
treated as "strangers" and at worst they encountered
racism) they found in the British churches.
Cultural togetherness. Black people have found themselves pushed together by their colour, attitudes towards

them and the law about them (the Nationality Bill). Categorised as an "ethnic minority" they have found strength in a shared life-style and belief.

Fission and fusion. The combined effect of reaction, cultural togetherness, splintering independence, the stress on personality leadership and embryonic structures has been to diversify and fragment.

According to Roswith Gerloff, the development has taken place in four phases:

Small, informal gatherings marked the early period as West Indian immigrants into London and Birmingham met in street and house meetings.

Denominalisation followed. Between 1953 and 1960 the main Churches were established – the New Testament Church of God, the Church of God Prophecy, the Church of God in Christ. Later, the First United Church of Jesus Christ (Apostolic), and the Pilgrim Wesleyan Holiness Church, followed. The Seventh Day Adventists, long established in the U.K., began to build up their multiracial committees.

Proliferation ran through the 1960s. Fission and fusions occurred according to the efficiency of leadership and participation, personality conflicts, class, geographical and national loyalties, and the racial, moral or financial policies of North American headquarters. Groups, even when doctrinally agreed, began fluttering around and starting new work. New names, including those of well-known, well-established black American Churches, became introduced into the British scene. Some Churches wished to preserve their West Indian values over against American infiltration and registered under the name of a West Indian indigenous movement. Others, in growing awareness of the racial question in a white society, split from white-dominated headquarters, became self-supporting, or joined black American headquarters. Some even tried to build up independent, if small, British organisations, in order to find ways and means to cross the

racial barriers and encounter "ecumenical" fellowship.
During this period the African Independent Church
Movement, through migration from Nigeria and Ghana,
came to Britain with the Church of the Lord Aladura,
Cherubim and Seraphim and the Ethiopian Orthodox
Church.

Strength and stability is the feature of the 1980s. An Afro-
Caribbean Church Council has been formed; joint
projects such as the Central Bible Institute in Birmingham
have drawn together white and black Christians; and a
magazine, *Exodus*, now gives a platform for news and
views from the black Churches. Many congregations now
have their own buildings, support paid leadership and are
linked into regional and national structures. Their
distinctive Gospel music has attracted great interest with
recordings and rallies reaching many British people.

These Churches have now reached a watershed. Younger
West Indians, with their personal experience of unemployment, racism and police harassment have been
influenced by the Black Power movement or the
Rastafarians, with their theology of cultural identity and
communal self-help. They now question what they
consider to be the escapism and pietism of their parents.
More thoughtful leaders are concerned about the necessity
for multi-racial congregations to portray oneness in a
divided society and the need to develop a wholeness of
approach that will address social and political concerns as
well as personal and inner hungers.

But even as this debate develops, other examples of
cultural congregations emerge in the inner city. Carib-
beans were followed by the Africans. Now South Asian
congregations are coming into being. They range from the
Mar Thoma Church (springing from the Syrian Orthodox
Church of South-West India) to the Pentecostal Asian
Communities. They carry a strong sense of belonging to a
community or caste which pervades the Church in South
Asia. Since they worship in their own language they retain
a clear-cut identity which will attract others from their

own culture but make a multi-racial, multi-national church very difficult to create. In this they have both opportunities and problems that are not known to the English-speaking congregations.

COMMUNITY OR FELLOWSHIP CHURCHES

Other churches have sprung from a shared desire to express the *Koinoinia*, or fellowship, themes of the New Testament. Vigorous worship, stress on life-style, personal evangelism, corporate leadership, and an impatience with the traditional, mainstream denominations mark these congregations. They are deeply influenced by the charismatic movement, strive to be multi-racial, are concerned with the reality of "principalities and powers" and are predominantly young in their membership.

Those known to me have come into being from a variety of situations. One is a house church that seeks to develop local leadership in the informal setting of a home and has created a "family" feeling for the thirty to forty members. Another is an offshoot from a para-church organisation which began with a committed cell of incoming young Christians and is now a strong, independent Church. Yet another is the gathering together of the disenchanted and the idealists in one area – a fall-out from traditional Churches.

Postively, these congregations carry a freshness and vitality much needed by the inner city. Their worship is open, has much participation, and is much longer than the more accepted patterns! A service will include a lot of singing, prayers, communion, sharing of news, a coffee break, a meal, preaching, greetings, embracing – the whole thing lasting for two to three hours. Their membership stresses body-ministry with the exercise of gifts.

Questions arise at several points. Too often the congregations can be unrepresentative, made up of incoming and transient young people and not really reaching the locals who watch from a distance. Their stress on personal faith, initial ignorace about the district in which they settle and uneasiness about the necessity to engage in the task of social transformation often prevents them from fully understanding, and entering into, the urban struggles going on around them. But they are there! Their vigour, togetherness and style of life is beginning to penetrate and influence pockets of the urban.

CHURCH PLANTING

In February, 1984, the London Baptist Association officers called a consultation on church planting. We faced the apparently inevitable decline of inner city congregations, and, in stark contrast, the stories of the strategic placing of a team of Baptist ministers, the work of Ichthus (a missionary agency in South London), the emergence of black and community churches, the concern of agencies like Youth for Christ and the surfacing of gifted individuals. The paradox of Church life in the inner city was set out. Churches were being planted in stony soil.

A wide variety of church planting techniques emerged. These included:

The prepared minister. A man or woman with theological training worked initially alongside an experienced pastor, then stayed within the team when going on to a struggling congregation. Baptist churches in East Ham, Hackney, Stratford, Leyton and Bow within the East London area were all involved in this approach – some beginning from the remnants of a once strong congregation, others from closure.

The gifted individual. A committed, concerned individual, with or without theological training, going to an area with an evangelistic concern. Often alone, this person begins work in a home and then moves on to congregational development.

The group. A small group commissioned from a larger

committed group. By 1983 Ichthus already had teams
operating in South London in resurrection (taking over
buildings where no work is taking place), co-operative
(work with very small "remnant" congregations) and new
(no building or congregation) settings.
The cultural. As in black-led churches, where a congregation grows out of the cultural identity of one ethnic
group.
The division. Where an existing congregation divides,
along theological or personality lines, and begins its own
life in another setting.
The agency. As in Youth for Christ or London City
Mission where, as purposeful strategy, a team, missionary
or officer is set aside and paid to initiate, yet remaining
within the support-structure of the agency. By 1981 at least
seventy-four missionaries from eight societies had returned from the mission field to work in the inner cities of
the U.K.

This is the latest wave of response to the missionary
mandate of Matthew 28. These efforts in London follow
on from the century-long saga of the building of parish
churches by the Anglicans, the combination of schools
and churches for the Roman Catholics, the establishment
of Settlements, the emergence of the Salvation Army, the
arrival of the London City Mission, the national network
of the Church Army, and the evangelistic efforts of Moody
and Sankey. Eleven new church Planting organisations
were known to be working in London in 1984 – in
addition to the denominations and traditional agencies.
  Some of the underlying issues of church planting in the
inner city have already emerged from different quarters.
While the Church movement can point to much success in
suburban areas it has had little impact on the inner city
and working parties have drawn out the lessons. These,
together with the insights and experience of those in the
field, are:

– The factors against Church growth in the inner city are

many and blatant. They are both contextual and institutional.

- The view that we should ignore the inner city people and concentrate resources on receptive areas is not an option for Christians.
- People in the inner city are reachable. Evidence now exists from many places of Church growth.
- The key problem is that of cross-cultural communication. The inner city is a mission field with its own distinct and varied cultures.
- The life-style of Christians and churches among the urban poor cannot and must not aim to be that of the white, middle class and suburban churches.
- Those with a gift for cross-cultural communication and a sense of calling should be set aside and trained for the work (probably by in-service methods and not at a theological college), should be supported by teams within the situation and, in turn, train others already there. The approaches will be varied and unconventional.
- The homogeneous unit congregation (such as a black church) is legitimate and authentic but it is never complete in itself and is therefore an interim model.

Much of the church planting activity stems from the Free Church traditions and the Anglican and Roman Catholic Churches find the movement difficult to appreciate. They begin with a parish model with a priestly centre. In theory, the spiritual needs of a geographical area should be met by the overall coverage of parish churches and the availability of the Body of Christ expressed in priest and people. But in practice, the coverage in the inner city is now geographically patchy, numerically weak and often too stereotyped, and points towards the need for a new Church for a new age. Black churches, community churches, church planting – all are "signs". Signs of a new reality and fresh life. They stand alongside older churches made new and relevant. They emerge like green shoots from a battered and semi-abandoned field.

NETWORKS

Back in 1981 I shared in an abortive attempt to list both the agencies and the literature of urban mission. We did reasonably well on the bibliography, using *The Inner City: A Connected Bibliography*, by Richard Farnell and published by the Shaftesbury Project. But the wave of publications compelled us to produce a new four-page document and the section on "Christian Perspectives" alone listed thirty-eight books or booklets. All but two had been published in the 1970s, indicating the pace and intensity of development. We struggled to list those Christian agencies known to be engaged in urban mission on a national basis.

At that time we were unable to find our way through a dense thicket of old and new. We were overwhelmed by:

The sheer size of the response – there were then over 200 black churches in London alone, sub-divided into at least thirty groupings.
The flux of the situation. Address changes, shift of aims, loss of funding, new issues – all conspired together to present a fluid, changing pattern.
The diversity of Christian reaction: Spanning evangelism and politics, containing individuals and congregations, set locally or planned nationally.
The patchiness of coverage. Merseyside seemed to have too much going on, Newcastle too little!
The hiddenness of much urban mission. Denominations often did not know what was going on. Non-denominational and local groups often had no national contact point.
The breaking of the wineskins. New life was springing out of the old.
The lack of definition. Urban and mission were two (and too) wide terms. Other words needed to be minted.

Many of the emerging patterns were, therefore, at first sight confusing. But within the complexity lay strands and themes. The green shoots began to join together to form a supporting, strengthening canopy of inter-locked networks. Networks were emerging in the 1970s but surfaced visibly around 1980/1.

Two major examples are C.O.S.P.E.C. – Christian Organisation for Social, Political and Economic Change; and E.C.U.M. – the Evangelical Coalition for Urban Mission. In January, 1980 nineteen groups came together to form C.O.S.P.E.C. They agreed a "Statement of Intent":

> C.O.S.P.E.C. is a federation of Christian groups and movements committed to co-operating in the struggle for a just, participatory and sustainable society.
>
> This will of necessity involve a break with the existing social, political and economic order.
>
> This end will be sought by joint action on matters of common concern, the sharing of our resources and national and regional network.

Later in 1980 Christian Action produced a *C.O.S.P.E.C. Agenda* which replaced *Christian Action Journal*, *The Christian Socialist*, *Christian Statesman*, *C.A.R.A.F. Newsletter*, *Movement*, *New City* and *The ONE Folder*. A network had emerged sailing under the insignia of the ecumenical movement. Committed to socialism, concerned with political justice, championing the minorities, facing national and international issues – C.O.S.P.E.C. drew together a movement of groups and organisations linked with, but critical of, the institutional Churches. While the movement is not exclusively centred on the urban poor, its impetus came from the inner city. Publications include the regular C.O.S.P.E.C. bulletin, *C.O.S.P.E.C. Stories* and a "Christian Political Manifesto" distributed from twenty-five centres.

The Evangelical Coalition for Urban Mission was launched in April 1981 and drew together five national groups whose genesis and approach were examples of the developing concern of evangelicals for urban mission. The covenanting bodies were:

- The Frontier Youth Trust which had sprung out of the Scripture Union. Serviced by six full-time officers, the F.Y.T. was concerned with young people on the frontiers of our society – youth clubs, detached workers, cells.
- The Evangelical Urban Training Programme began in 1974 and works to develop local leadership in working class communities through a national director in Merseyside and regional workshops.
- *Christians in Industrial Areas* – a correspondence magazine for those interested in working in the inner cities or overspill estates of urban Britain.
- The Evangelical Race Relations Group (now Evangelical Christians for Racial Justice) was wrestling with racism, encouraging partnership between black and white Christians, and studying the interaction of people of different ethnic groups in Britain.
- Shaftesbury Project – Inner City Group is part of a research analysis team producing papers like "Powerlessness in the Inner City."

With bases in London, Liverpool, Birmingham and Nottingham stretching out through regional workshops and committees to cover the whole of the U.K., these groups drew together a new generation of evangelicals, many from the radical discipleship wing, who are concerned about the cultural and spiritual implications of traditional evangelicalism. At the heart of E.C.U.M. there is a "fraternity" of those who, from an evangelical background, but from widely differing situations and spheres of interest, find that they have been brought to a similar vision and concern which is expressed in the manifesto. Out of their concern for both personal faith and social justice has come the periodical *City Cries*, a directory of agencies engaged in urban mission, a regular E.C.U.M. bulletin and a series of workshops and conferences gathering, co-ordinating, and initiating work in the inner city.

Both C.O.S.P.E.C. and E.C.U.M. are networks linking across denominational and geographical lines, drawing together the insights and contributions of Christians concerned about the Gospel and society. While C.O.S.P.E.C. has a wider and more political brief, E.C.U.M. is rooted within the urban areas of the U.K.

Other national networks which include the inner cities and council estates are N.A.C.C.A.N. (National Centre for Christian Communities and Networks), Jubilee (a largely Anglo-Catholic grouping), and at least two organisations gathering together the black churches.

THE MODEL

In the *total mission* of the Church, a wide range of Christian groups and agencies now operate among the urban poor. These include:

- Social action groups.
- Support and sharing groups operating on a "care and share" basis, and drawing individuals into group life.
- Development groups with a stress on wholeness.
- Renewal programmes establishing locally controlled, often co-operative services to maintain economic independence.
- Cell-groups coming together to develop a deeper, indigenous, urban spirituality.
- The spreading of the simple life-style movement.
- New forms of training for both professional and lay members of the Church.
- The deliberate entry of Christians into the worlds of labour, politics and economics.

In the *Evangelistic task*, signs of hope both in numerical growth and widening outreach can be seen in:

- The emergence in force of black-led Churches.
- The rich diversity of para-denominational Churches, including house fellowships.
- The committed concern of agencies like the Scripture Union, the Church Army and Youth for Christ for the inner city situation.

The focal point of all these signs of hope, whether in the broader sweep of mission or the specific task of evangelism, is to be found in one model – *Base communities*. This is not a British or European discovery. The workshop on Christian Witness to the Urban Poor at the Consultation on World Evangelism in 1980, drawn from six sub-continents, concluded:

> We believe the basic strategy for the evangelisation of the urban poor is the creation or renewal of communities in which Christians live and share equally with others. These communities function as a holistic redemptive presence among the poor, operate under indigenous leadership, demonstrate God's love and invite men, women and children to repentance, faith and participation in God's Kingdom.

Three reasons lie behind this belief: current experience, social rightness and biblical pattern.

Current experience indicates that evangelistic work begins with the building up of small communities or cells. In Brazil alone there are more than 80,000 "base communities" with over 2,000,000 people, largely rooted in Catholicism. Evangelical experiences in places like Hong Kong where, through such communities, 600 people within ten years have been drawn to Christ from amongst the poorest workers. And in the U.K. small, newly planted churches are growing up to cover people of many cultures and ethnic origins, using homes and the "base community" as the fundamental feature. Established Churches find renewal through the new life springing from the cells now to be found in many denominations and areas.

Social rightness confirms the model. The base communities convey the possibility of caring, healing, integration and purpose to those who have known hopelessness. Where economic pressures have affected the individual's capacity to make choices or decisions an accepting and affirming group will encourage the development of gifts and the confidence required to face responsibility. As in a human family, this can only take place within a nurturing environment. In such a caring community, the way of Christ as a living reality will become a genuine option for the poor. Although the groups vary in form and style, they will become a redemptive presence, demonstrating God's love. The base community puts faith at street level.

The biblical pattern is that "the Word is made flesh." Faith, hope and love are to be experienced and shared. Base communities embody and express the Gospel. Within them, relevant Bible Study and corporate prayer tie in with the everyday realities of life. Through them, joyful participation in worship, new styles of living within simplicity and stewardship plus directness in evangelism confront neighbours and friends.

These base communities have largely displaced traditional programmes in Church life among the urban poor. Women's Meetings, uniformed organisations and central prayer meetings have largely disappeared. The "gathered community" of the Free Churches in which I grew up was largely centred on a building and a minister and an accepted liturgy. All the thriving Churches I now know are built upon the small groups that centre faith and come together in the wider congregational worship – many are without their own buildings or paid, professional leadership.

They have different names: Root Groups, Family Fellowships, Vine Groups, Communities of Faith, Grassroot Communities. But whatever the name, these groups answer deep-seated human needs. They provide a new understanding of being human in the context of poverty and injustice as personal relationships give value to the rejected. They offer a new model of the Church which does not require expensive buildings or a professional ministry but uses homes and builds an indigenous leadership. They create a shared ministry, drawing out gifts and enriching the larger, congregational services. They are a new way of doing theology as they hold together everyday realities and the Scriptures, working from the bottom up. They give a new understanding of mission as they proclaim the Good News in words, being and action.

The setting-up of base communities can begin either from the policy of a local church or the expressed needs of a group of Christians. A "pastoral agent" will be needed to focus and initiate the group. A suitable base in an open, caring home will be required. A balance of celebration, prayer, discussion and refreshment must be kept. The "two-legged" approach of Scriptue-reality is central.

There are problems to be faced. These include the dilemma of being very local and yet needing to keep a larger perspective; the danger of isolation; the uneasy relationships with established Churches; the temptation to prefer self-expression in discussion to obedience to the Scriptures; the reluctance to face structural and institutional demands; the lapsing into pietism.

But the base Christian community is here to stay. It is important because it seeks to be a microcosm of what Church *and* society should be like. It is strategic because it provides a building block, the small group, for the larger structures. It is radical because it starts at the roots of human life. It is evangelistic because it is a visual aid to the Gospel and a doorway for the seeker. It serves the urban poor because it is *of* them and *for* them. It is both biblical and contemporary.

POSTSCRIPT

I know that this array of activity is as bewildering to those outside the inner cities as it is exciting to those inside. Those of us who have been witnesses to the unfolding pattern that began with committed individuals and small groups, surfaced in the variety of projects concerned with social transformation, led on to a wave of new churches, grew together in the networks and finds an anchorage in the basic community – we have had time and experience to educate us. I also know how patchy these signs of hope are, more evident in some parts than in others.

Whatever else they may be, and however they develop in the future, they are nonetheless deeply significant to British Christians. They are pointers beyond themselves to both the hurts and the healing of the inner city. Small as they are, they are prophetic in their very existence – telling out the concern of God for the oppressed and the struggling, and embodying the fruit of the Spirit. Each sign has emerged with birth pangs and hurt and they are to be seen as one part of the continuing struggle on this earth between the Kingdom of God and the power of darkness.

8

THE STRUGGLE

Drive in the traffic at the heart of any British city in the rush hour. It moves. It stops. The peculiar mixture of stop and go with the attendant emotions of frustration and hope can be paralleled in urban ministry. In both traffic and ministry there is flow and hold-up, a sense of movement and then a depressing slow-down.

Writing a book like this gives a vantage point on a bridge above the traffic, knowing what it feels like to be down there yet gaining a perspective from the over-view. From this angle the signs of hope and the stumbling blocks can be seen to intermingle.

Looking back over twenty years within the urban environment, I can see clearly the growth and the new life. But I can also see the other side of the story – the recurrence of old sores.

Concentrate on the positive and you have an unreal, superficial optimism. Burdened by the negative you will feel overwhelmed, despairing and impotent. Put together the positives and the negatives and they form a series of couplets which pinpoint the hopes we share and the blocks we face in urban mission:

AWARENESS – IGNORANCE
NEW LIFE – OLD SORES
RESOURCES – EXCUSES
TOTAL MINISTRY – CLERGY DOMINATION
"PRINCIPALITIES AND POWERS" – STRUCTURAL SIN
PLURALISM – RACISM
SOCIAL TRANSFORMATION – SELF-CENTRED FAITH

AWARENESS AND IGNORANCE

In the U.K. we have been awakened to the plight of
the urban poor by the steady out-pouring of research
and writings and by the volcanic eruption of the 1981
riots.

As Christians, we now know that we have a massive
national problem, whether we see it as a mission field
requiring evangelists, a battlefield needing healing and
reconciliation, or a ghetto crying out for justice. We have
heard about accelerating unemployment, the build-up of
racial tension, the accusations of police insensitivity, the
withdrawal of the educated, the pervading sense of
powerlessness, multiple deprivation and political provo-
cation by the extremists.

But there is still widespread ignorance. Much of it is
inevitable, because the courses of our lives take us to
different places. But the ignorance that is a real block is
that of attitude rather than knowledge. It is the view that
the urban poor deserve what they get. It is the power of
vested interests, the "what we have we hold" philosophy,
and the moral confusion about poverty as fate, blessedness
or scandal. It is, above all, the failure of compassion and
the evasion of justice. It is the not *wanting* to know that is
the real enemy.

NEW LIFE AND OLD SORES

One of the most powerful signs of hope in the urban scene
is the persistent thrust of new life. It can easily seem lost in
the dust or buried among the paper! But it can be found in
the apparently secular organisations as well as in the
Churches. I look around me in East London to see a
Parent's Centre drawing out energy and commitment
from local homes, a Renewal Programme utilising
abandoned churches, Community Links operating from a
shop-front. I work with lively, initiating people who

bring music, drama, organisation and caring to the community.

I see the new life of the Kingdom within and often initiating the new life of our society. Alongside *New Society*, *New Statesman* and the *New Scientist* goes the *New World of Missions*, the *Church Growth Digest* and *Third Way*.

Yet the sins of 1 Corinthians – personality cults, division, dispute and exclusivism – have their counterparts today. The Wheaton '83 conference sponsored by the World Evangelical Fellowship and gathering 300 people from sixty countries to consider the "nature and mission of the Church" said in its letter to the Churches:

> We are sad to learn ... that there are sometimes serious tensions between churches and para-church agencies. We humbly appeal to everybody involved to be responsible stewards to what God has entrusted to us. Let us therefore be mindful of each other and together listen to our Lord. Only in this way will our time, resources and personnel be used responsibly and will we strengthen each other in our common ministry. And only so can the friction caused by paternalism, insensitivity, and abuse of power be overcome.

Alongside the new life of the urban, often so fragile and vulnerable, come the sapping, life-destroying sores that spring from our self-centredness and sin. Repentance, like Judgement, has to begin in the household of God; "Do not restrain the Holy Spirit" was not written solely for the Thessalonians.

RESOURCES AND EXCUSES

The Christian Church has a tremendous reservoir of resources. Yet so often both policy and personal decisions have led to a withdrawal of resources from the very areas which need them most.

Only the Government and local authorities have comparable resources in terms of buildings. Buildings are "spiritual signs and vehicles of mission" and there is much that offers hope in the way buildings are being used today. Increased accessibility to the community, imaginative reconstruction, wider usage and bold projects can all be found. But as we have explored, there is still bad use made of church buildings, not least the unhealthy desire to cling on to the past.

When we turn to personnel there is much evidence of personal and sacrificial commitment. Individualism is giving way to the broader team approaches. Preparation for leadership roles is using both induction (for those coming in) and contextual (within the situation) methods. Emphasis is moving from the ordained to the lay, from the individual to the corporate, from incomers to the indigenous and from the "parachute" short-stay to the long-term "seed in the ground" approach.

But two durable blocks continue to exist. The ordained ministry is often reluctant to come and the lay people are often too quick to move. When I first arrived in West Ham in 1965 I used to meet fellow-ministers who quickly told me how eager they were to work in the inner city but their concern for the education of their children prevented them from doing so. Twenty years on that reason has been removed but only one of my friends has taken the opportunity to come to the inner city! On the other side, I am constantly bemused by the way local Christians will pray for guidance on Church affairs but accept, without prayer or consultation, the generally held view that "it is a good thing to move out."

The agencies sponsored by the Church to meet the needs of the inner cities from the late nineteenth century are all going through trauma that will lead to new life or to extinction. Groups like the Church Army have faced a commission into their future, the Shaftesbury Society has looked hard at its policy for missions, and the City Missions are taking stock. New agencies have sprung up which is enormously encouraging, but there is another

side. Some agencies, such as The Salvation Army, seem to
be unable to reverse their withdrawal from the inner cities.
It is a paradox that the movement which began in East
London is now numerically at its weakest there. Other
agencies fall prey to hardening of the arteries and loss of
vitality. A preoccupation with status rather than service,
programme rather than people and continuation rather
than change are the presented symptoms of inner disease.

In financial terms, there is evidence of hope. Local
generosity is matched with denominational concern. The
Baptists began a deliberate redeployment of their Home
Mission Fund towards the urban poor with grants to an
ecumenical project in Salford and a London E.C.U.M.
network. The Methodists launched a Mission Alongside
the Poor fund and set out to raise a million pounds. The
Anglicans, in a survey on "The Historic Resources of the
Church of England" began to face "the apparently
inequitable distribution of monies available to each diocese
from historic and other sources". Chritians were path-
finders in utilising wider funding from Government
schemes like Urban Aid, Partnership Schemes or through
their local authorities. Financial resources on an unprecedented scale have been made available through the
Housing Associations, the Manpower Services Commission and the Commission for Racial Equality. An even
more far-reaching sign of hope was the decision by Oxfam
in 1984 to aid urban projects in Manchester and
Edinburgh, thereby underscoring the links between
poverty and underdevelopment in this country and
overseas.

But the stumbling blocks are prominent. The report of a
working party set up by the Diocesan Synod of Liverpool
in 1982 pointed out two unfair burdens on urban priority
areas:

The financial demands made by Stipend assessments,
quota, housing costs and plant maintenance severely
inhibit the church's mission in priority areas ... A high
proportion of church members and potential members

depend on social security, average incomes are low, church attendance and financial support is often small in comparison with other areas, donations in kind are less frequent, overhead costs (such as insurance) are often higher.

The entrenched strength of the historical rootage of finance (as in benefices) militates against the newer, less well-endowed urban areas. The suburban access to resources from the better-off is seen both in the ready availability of money and access to the financial networks that provide both know-how and resources.

Everywhere I look I see a struggle going on about the use of resources – whether it be in buildings, personnel, agencies or money.

TOTAL MINISTRY AND CLERGY DOMINATION

The stress on indigenous leadership now encourages and allows more local people to share in the running of the Church but the persisting style (committees, paper) prevents the full utilisation of the gifts of those who know the area. The arrival of incomers is in this regard a mixed blessing in that the youthfulness and vitality of those coming in can lead to insensitivity to the skills and commitments of the indigenous. But the role and training of the clergy is still seen as the real key, and is often a major stumbling block.

One of the aims of the Archbishop's Commission is: "To gather information; evaluate and commend effective forms of mission and ministry; and to identify necessary developments and training in a rapidly changing society".[1]

We have at present a real and apparently irreconcilable conflict between two models of ministry. Model A is the traditional, historical view of the church functioning around a central professional leader who is imported into the local situation. He is accorded a status and title and becomes, with success, a messiah-figure; or, with failure, a scape-goat.

Model B starts from the congregation and has a participating, gift-accepting style that draws out and builds on the strength of all the members. It is seen at its simplest in the base community but it flows into the larger worship congregations and the overall mission of the Church. Here there is much untidiness but more sharing.

The tension between the two models, both of which claim scriptural justification, centres around expectations. What are the expectations carried within the leader-pastor, preacher, enabler? What are the expectations held by the congregation – to be looked after or to be encouraged to participate?

There is another problem with the professional ministry of the Church among the urban poor. Stipendiary clergy are drawn from the middle class. They are largely trained on academic lines and often impose alien patterns. Even those going to theological colleges from the urban poor (and they are few indeed!) are considered to be "starched" as they grow away from their peer group. Two approaches to this problem are currently in favour: induction and contextual training. Induction takes a trained man and introduces him to the history and present realities of the urban environment before a ministry commences. Contextual training seeks to discern men and women with leadership potential already in the urban setting and to prepare them within their context by a process of action and reflection.

But more serious by far than the problems of training methods or cultural gaps is the question of attitudes. One of my own friends in the Baptist ministry honestly and movingly set this out when he wrote in his church magazine about his move from an inner city church to a suburban congregation:

Those with good memories are perhaps wondering how all this can be reconciled with my scepticism at times about ministers claiming to be "led" when usually they move to pleasanter places and rarely the reverse. I have concluded that most of us set some limits on our openness to God's guidance and, although I am not proud of doing so, I think it is more honest to confess it. As it happens Pinner comes quite outside my expectations but I suspect that, because it is a pleasant place, it will be easier than what I really feel I should have been open to, namely a struggling inner city church in an area of urban deprivation. Yet I didn't feel at this point that I had the courage, the faith or the energy to cope with it. Nevertheless it is on my conscience and I believe it should be on my agenda for the future![2]

That sort of honesty is rare as is the succinct letter one U.R.C. leader wrote in 1981 in response to the Nationwide Initiative of Evangelism booklet on "The Urban Poor": "Provision of ministry for the work in the church of the urban poor can only be at the expense of the ministry presently provided elsewhere. As is so often the case, what is required is neither administrative flair, nor imagination, but sacrifice."

Nowhere do the signs of hope and the stumbling blocks jar so obviously and significantly as in the realm of leadership. It is here that one of the key fulcrums of change and renewal will either develop or be blocked.

THE KINGDOM OF GOD AND "PRINCIPALITIES AND POWERS"

Anyone reflecting deeply on the process of attrition, the breakdown of effort, the sense of impotence and the apparent failure of the Kingdom of God in the inner cities is brought face to face with Paul's words to the Ephesians: "For we are not fighting against human beings but against the wicked spiritual forces in the heavenly world, the rulers, authorities, and cosmic power of this dark age" (Eph. 6:12).

When a National Front cordon was stretched across the front of Lawrence Hall to block a meeting of black people I glimpsed behind the chanting and the hostility something of the intimidating power of evil that has to do with far more than personal sin. There are powers at work in the structures of society which oppress and crush human beings. We are all sinners but some are more sinned against than sinning. It is a sign of hope that Christians can talk directly and honestly about "principalities and powers". The E.C.U.M. Manifesto calls upon Christians "To identify and challenge in Christ's name, the oppressive and demonic in individuals, communities and institutions."

David Watson, in his preface to *Rich Christians in an Age of Hunger* by Ronald Sider, commented: "Repentance for personal sin is not enough. As the prophets make clear, we need to repent also for the structural evil in society; and any genuine repentance will lead to a serious attempt to change those structures which encourage the evil."

Leslie Crosland's paper *Principalities, Power and Social Structures* grew out of the Inner City Group of the Shaftesbury Project. He points out that the biblical references suggest questions of political and social impotence and that the concept of "principalities and powers" is a useful tool for Christians concerned with a biblical analysis of society.

My own belief is that we have only just begun to grapple with this theme and that it will loom ever larger on the agenda for the future. We have failed to comprehend the awe-fulness of the "principalities and powers". The only conference I have ever attended that saw all sections ending in silence was the British Council of Churches consultation on Poverty in 1984. There the groups, workshops and finally the full consultation stumbled into silence in the face of the massive forces we met within poverty and injustice and what this meant to our own beliefs and life-styles.

Sometimes I feel it is like an impersonal, unfeeling, malevolent tide remorselessly creeping in. I grow increasingly aware of the struggle between the Kingdom of Light and the Kingdom of Darkness and I believe the inner city is one of the central battlegrounds.

PLURALISM AND RACISM

In their booklet *Christian Community and Cultural Diversity* Barbara Holden and Eric Rolls describe Britain's multiracial and multi-faith society:

> In the last thirty years the shape of British Society has changed. Not everywhere has felt the impact of this change in the same way. While it is possible to sit on the top deck of a London bus and hear for mile after mile never a word of English, it is equally possible to visit some rural community whether in Lincolnshire or Cornwall where there has never yet set foot anybody of Asian or African origin. Even in a city like Leeds or Bradford it is perfectly possible to go over the brow of a hill and there to find that the outer suburb reflects nothing of the mixing of races and cultures and religious grouping that its neighbouring inner city area so obviously indicates.

This massive influx of people and the subsequent social adjustments have created a volatile atmosphere within which signs of hope and stumbling blocks are at their most extreme. The black presence has become the barium meal of British society – revealing that which was already present, showing up the inner disease.

On one side, the pluralist society gives an opportunity for a cosmopolitan and rich diversity of cultures and attitudes. On the other hand, Empire attitudes, competing claims for territory, and the concentration of immigrants in narrow bands has led to racism, hostility and division.

For Christians, the biblical dream of Paul: "There is no difference between Jews and Gentiles, between slaves and free men, between men and women; you are all one in union with Christ Jesus" (Gal. 3:28); and the Book of Revelation: "After this I looked, and there was an enormous crowd – no one could count all the people!

They were from every race, tribe, nation, and language, and they stood in front of the throne of the Lamb . . .'' (Rev. 7:9) are still utopian and distant.

We have congregations where black and white mingle together but few are genuinely at one. We have partnerships between black and white Churches in projects like Zebra but they are few in number. The British Council of Churches has published *Coming Together in Christ, Building Together in Christ*, and *Learning in Partnership* but the very titles indicate the needs. We have a wave of ethnic or cultural congregations impelling the British Church Growth Association to publish *Christian Ethnics: Church Growth in Multi-Cultural Britain*. These congregations arouse in me contrasting emotions of delight and unease. I delight in the whole-heartedness of their worship, their passion for evangelism and their love for each other; I am uneasy at the fragmentation of Christ's Church, the failure to respond to the needs of their own young people (unemployment, hostility and identity) and the continuation of the gaps between the congregation and society.

If the scenario were Christian alone there would still be confusion. But urban immigrants have brought with them their own religions, so the problem has escalated: we have a multi-faith, multi-racial, multi-cultural melting pot – and this is centred in the inner cities. Walking across Regent's Park in central London the sight of the gold dome of the Mosque still surprises. Driving into East London the brand-new, imposing mosque in the Commercial Road is virtually opposite the General Booth Centre for the Homeless and is a stinging shock for many Christians. The Union of Muslims Organisation now claims a Muslim community of over 1,500,000 in Britain; these came from Pakistan and Bangladesh, from the Near and Middle East, from Africa, from Malaysia and from the Caribbean. There are approximately 250,000 Hindus and 200,000 Sikhs in Britain now, mostly in the large cities. There are no reliable figures for Buddhism but the figure could be as high as 100,000 especially since the second largest ethnic community in Britain comprises the Chinese and the Vietnamese boat people. We also have the much smaller communities of Baha'is, Jains and Zoroastrians with several thousands of members each.

The level of religious adherence within these community figures is hard to assess but the cultural identity is a potent force. All face the same struggles that Christianity knows: the falling away of young people and the effects of the "acids of modernity". All now include white British people among their numbers.

The Churches have responded to this religious pluralism in a variety of ways. Committees, theological projects, centres for study and publications have tackled "other faiths". One of the best introductory publications is by the U.R.C.: *With People of Other Faiths in Britain: A Study Handbook for Christians.*

The British Council of Churches stresses the need for dialogue. Dialogue begins when people meet each other, it depends upon mutual understanding and trust, makes it possible to share in service to the community, and can become the medium of authentic witness.

It is at the point of "authentic witness" that Christians in the U.K. face a series of connected and awkward questions. What is the place of other religions in the economy of God? How do we understand "there is no other name..."? How do we support an ethnic community and yet seek individual converts? Even if the questions can be answered our lack of understanding of other faiths and the weakness of our missionary zeal militates against creative or urgent response.

Stronger by far than all the other stumbling blocks in the multi-racial field is the deep-seated prevalence of racism. It is not new. Back in 1924, J. H. Oldham published *Christianity and the Race Problem.* Racism is entrenched in British society and experienced at many levels. Racism is hidden in social structures as well as carried by the individual – it is prejudice plus power. Racism is a colonial legacy, a master–slave approach, built on superiority/inferiority, fuelled by fear and totally alien to the Christian belief in the worth and dignity of each human before God. It is an ugly, destructive attitude which is sadly found in the Churches – and it is certainly one of the reasons why black Churches have emerged. It is in all white people. It is an insidious, pervading attitude which I know within myself, and see in the attitudes of others but which is experienced most personally and poignantly by those whose skin is not white. In Tony Ottey's vivid picture: "It may be that blacks are on the same boat as poor whites, but they are on different decks."

A series of cameos we have seen in and around us at Lawrence Hall illustrates the way that racism leads to violence, deceit, and political furore:

It took three of the staff here to prevent an incensed white lad attacking a limited, inoffensive black lad after a misunderstanding...

The National Front booked one of our halls under the name of the East London Model Railway Society...

The group East London Workers against Racism was besieged in our premises by a coachload of National Front members...

The first eviction by a local authority of a tenant from a white home for racial harassment in January 1985 meant the Housing Chairman required a police escort...

SOCIAL TRANSFORMATION AND SELF-CENTRED FAITH

There is a deep-rooted uncertainty in British Christianity about social issues, especially where these have political overtones. The debate about the nature of the Kingdom of God, the traditional evangelical unease about the "social Gospel" and, above all, the belief that faith is only a matter between the Creator and the created have all left unresolved questions.

Some of these questions are being raised by Christians working in the urban/industrial areas. The Urban Theology Unit in Sheffield set out "To contribute to the creation of a theology in Britain which will constitute an adequate response to the social and political realities of our time, and which will help Christians in their search for suitable patterns of action."

A far-reaching transformation is occurring among evangelical Christians. After a time of neglect evangelicals are returning to the wholeness of Wesley, Wilberforce and Finney. Evangelism and social concern are again seen to be complementary and interrelated rather than competitive and divisive. In the words of David Watson, "Evangelism and social action are the two blades of a pair of scissors; if we have one without the other we lose our cutting edge."[3]

The word "transformation" has surfaced as a preferable alternative to the terms "relief" or "development" which are associated with the assumption that poverty and hunger are only the result of ignorance and backwardness rather than oppressive, unjust social structures. By using the word "transformation" evangelicals accept the view that the reduction of poverty and powerlessness will require not just new technology and better information but also the correction of structural injustice.

The running together of two streams – the traditional concern for society and the scripturally based concern of the evangelicals – has created a strong-flowing river. It can be seen in the changing attitudes of Christians, the emergence of issue-centred projects, political involvement, self-help groups, community centres, and a wide range of action groups. Yet there is still a long way to go. Try a test in any congregation. Practically everyone will chorus the opening words of Psalm twenty-three: "The Lord is my Shepherd." Ask for the first sentence of Psalm twenty-four and you'll get a silence before a single voice responds, "The earth is the Lord's." An exploration of why we know Psalm twenty-three but not Psalm twenty-four has to go beyond usage and sentiment; it must include the fact that personal faith sticks at that point. Full faith has to undergo three conversions: conversion to Jesus Christ, which is the fundamental, life-changing, inner transaction of faith; conversion to the Church as the body, fellowship and vehicle of the Gospel; conversion to the world as the created arena in which the Holy Spirit is forever working in the personalities, institutions and nations of humankind. To stop at the first is to stay forever in a truncated self-centredness; to remain at the second is to live within a spiritual ghetto; to hold all three together is the biblical way which is holistic and purposive.

9

THE UNDERLYING QUESTION

HIDDEN BUT HAUNTING

In 1979 I went to look at the inner cities of the U.S.A. Just before I left Britain I completed a doctoral thesis on "The Inter-action of Church and Society in an East London Borough." That research was the story of what had happened to one urban community, West Ham, and to the Church within it. But even as I handed it in I was uneasily aware that something remained unanswered. Something still lay hidden below the surface.

While I was in Washington I discovered a booklet with the title *To Hear and to Heed*. It was published by the Urban Bishops' Coalition of the Episcopal Church and was a summary of the hearings held in a series of cities. It was compelling reading, an eloquent and impassioned plea for understanding and action. But in my mind the impasse still remained. The same feeling persisted. It was like a mediaeval palimpsest, a manuscript which had been over-written with a message which hid the original.

Slowly it dawned on me. Underneath our human concern and analysis, behind our experiments and projects lay the pattern of human life as intended by God, set out in the Scriptures and focussed in Jesus Christ – and so often ignored, even by Christians. The covering-up and the accretions, however skilful and impressive, could not obscure the deeper realities which must eventually break through: God's purpose and human sin; God's grace and His people; God's justice and His world plan.

Were Christians really different in their attitudes and life-style from non-Christians? How far had the Church faced, and grasped, the wholeness of Scripture? In short, how far had the Kingdom, or rule, of God become embodied and made real in the people of Christ?

I know I ought to have seen this much earlier in my pilgrimage. The whole story of our efforts to "make the Word flesh" ought to have brought out the central question. Certainly the sharpness of the insights of the Third World and the mounting stress signals within our own country should have pierced my defences.

For me, it came late on in life, this question that lies right at the core of the life of the urban, and right at the heart of the life of the disciples of Jesus. An insistent "I refuse to be silenced" question that pushes me back to the One who exemplified in Himself the Kingdom.

The underlying question haunts me. It has yet to be fully answered. It is an awkward, unsettling, ever-present mirror. It has to do with God's concern for the oppressed, the powerless and the deprived, and His answer in the incarnation and life of Jesus Christ. It stresses the wholeness of the Gospel. It points to a corporate solidarity instead of the individualism we practise.

THE PROCESS OF DEFLECTION

Three things prevented me – and I believe others – from receiving the deeper message. They are lack of an over-view, selectivity and spiritualisation.

Many pieces from the Bible were in my head, but always in snippets or sections. I jumped from rock to rock without seeing the thrust and depth of the stream. It was the riots of 1981 that revealed this. The editor of the Baptist Times asked for a series of articles about "the message from the inner cities". It was not difficult to relay the frustrations and fears reflected in the anger and violence. Nor was it hard to string together extracts from the many letters and statements from Christian Churches and groups involved in the situation. What was difficult was the scriptural response to the turmoil. For the first time for years, I read right through the Bible and found a clear message coming through about God's concern for the oppressed and the powerless. This concern was carried in the Old Testament teachings about community life and proclaimed by the prophets. In the New Testament it found its earthing in the coming of Jesus, His life-style and teaching and was embodied in the emergence of the Church as the people of God.

This meant that I had been selective in my understanding. Whole slabs of the Bible had failed to register. I knew the Ten Commandments were in Exodus 20 but I had never heard of the Jubilee principle of Leviticus 25. Since boyhood I had lived with the Great Commission of Matthew 28:16-20 but had never faced the Nazareth manifesto of Luke 4:18-19. I had been blinkered, blinded and bereft – and I asked "why?"

That answer came when I saw the all-enveloping grip of our spiritualisation of the Bible. This is a side-stepping process that allows us to keep the words but to change the meaning. Take the word peace (*shalom*). I grew up with the idea that this meant an inner experience, a peace with God. Now I know that *shalom* means wholeness and harmony at every level of human life: material welfare, and prosperity. The community is the proper setting for *shalom* and social relationships express the outworking of it. God's *shalom* comes when an individual is one within him or herself, with other people, and with God. That is the harmony God wants.

Look at salvation. Salvation in the Bible was seen as liberation from oppression into an uncramped environment and was primarily communal, social and political. This is illustrated repeatedly by the Exodus from the bondage of Egypt into the liberty of the Promised Land, but it has been spiritualised into a private, other-worldly deliverance.

It took a layman to open my eyes to this. Roger Dowley, a solicitor who, with his wife Ruth, has chosen to live first in Bow and then in Camberwell hammered out the full meaning of basic scriptural themes like salvation, *shalom*, righteousness, redeemer, covenant and Messiah in his book *Towards the Recovery of a Lost Bequest*. In another of his writings he focusses on:

> ... the persistent tendency for those with power and resources to take over for themselves the benefits of God's grace to the exclusion of the poor and oppressed. This tendency was discernible throughout the Old Testament and was condemned by the prophets, it was operating in Gospel times and was condemned by Jesus and it has been present throughout the Christian era and rarely condemned, but usually tolerated.
>
> To the comfortably-placed holding the reins of power, the proclamation of a just and righteous society of *Shalom* for all men, with a bias towards the poor, is a continuing obstacle and embarrassment – so they exert their power to mute the proclamation until it's this-worldly application is silenced. Having themselves no need of a this-worldly liberation and feeling threatened by its being proclaimed to those who do feel such a need, they encourage and stimulate spiritualised other-worldly intepretations which leave undisturbed and unchallenged the injustice in the social status quo.

That I found to be uncomfortably true of myself and of all that I could see and hear within much of the Christian Church.

A discussion in our coffee bar one evening with a group of young Marxists focussed on the words justice and oppression. They had assumed that those were Marxist political terms and were astonished to learn that the Bible actually used the phrases! An impromptu Bible-study revealed both Marxist ignorance and Christian failure to communicate. Beneath the failure is a whole process of spiritualisation and avoidance which lifts Bible words out of earthiness and into the ethereal:

Peace has shifted from wholeness to inner serenity; *Salvation* has become personalised; *Poverty* has been

moved from physical deprivation to spiritual impoverishment; *Justice* has been quietly dropped; *Covenant* has
been made unilateral; and *Torah (Law)* has been avoided.

It is a sign of hope that an increasing number of
Christians struggle with the whole Gospel for the whole of
life and refuse to allow compartmentalised life-spheres or
the "privatisation of religion". It is a sign of hope that
more understand that in the Bible, economic and
ecological issues are spiritual issues, and vice-versa.

But it would be unwise to underestimate the stumbling
blocks. There is a great tenacity in the way we hear the
things we only want to hear. The signs of hope are
glimmers, yet to be accepted and worked out. We have lost
something on the way. There is a process, a downward
tug. There is a deflection and an evasion. It is right at the
root of what is wrong with us, the Church, and the world.
It has to do with the old-fashioned word disobedience.
When Jesus said, "You will always have poor people with
you" (Mark 14:7), he was pointing out that we are sinful in
permitting poverty. For his words are a quotation from the
Old Testament: "Not one of your people will be poor if
you obey me" (Deut. 15:4-5).

ILLUSTRATED BY "POOR"

In 1980 I was asked to draw together a paper from the U.K.
on the "urban poor" in preparation for the Consultation
on World Evangelisation. Jim Punton, the training
officer of the Frontier Youth Trust, had undertaken to
prepare a document on the biblical words for "poor". As
we flew over Israel on our way to Thailand he tossed it into
my lap. As I scanned page after page of references I felt as if
I was walking through an avalanche. I dodged the first
stones, was knocked over by the next wave and was finally
swept away by the cumulative force of hundreds of
references. I had not known how much the Bible said
about the poor – in the Old Testament alone there are nine
different words in 300 references. Somewhere along the
line my upbringing, training and personal attitudes had

combined to prevent me seeing and hearing.

One of the most difficult, yet rewarding, tasks I have ever done was the final editing of the Thailand Report No. 22: *Christian Witness to the Urban Poor*. In that booklet you will find a full recording and analysis of the words for "poor" drawn up by Jim Punton. One section – the Bible and the Poor – was central to the thinking of the group that met in Pattaya and much that follows is taken from the wrestling and insights of that group. Work through it with a Bible beside you.

In the Old Testament, "poor" can be translated by six major and three other terms, totalling about 300 references, and revealing a broad understanding of the causes, reality and consequences of poverty. The poor person is the down-trodden, humiliated, oppressed; the man pleading and crying out for justice; the weak or helpless; the destitute; the needy, dependent person; and the one forcibly subjected to the powerful oppressor. The wide range of terms shows that "the poor" must be seen from many perspectives. Clustering around "the poor" are linked words like the "widow", the "fatherless" and the "stranger".

The New Testament uses a number of terms to describe the poor: the manual worker who struggles to survive on a day-to-day basis; the destitute cowering as a beggar; the one reduced to "meekness"; the one brought low. We must include those weakened and exhausted by heavy burdens, the leper and the "common people".

Throughout the Bible the majority of references indicate that the poor are the mercilessly oppressed and the downtrodden. Nor is their poverty taken for granted in Scripture. It causes concern, anger and protest. It is challenged and opposed. And its source is seen as injustice and oppression by the powerful.

Right at the beginning of his ministry Jesus declared in the synagogue of Nazareth that the words of the ancient prophet had come to fulfilment: "The Spirit of the Lord is upon me, because he has chosen me to bring good news to the poor. He has sent me to proclaim liberty to the captives and recovery of sight to the blind; to set free the oppressed and announce that the time has come when the Lord will save his people" (Luke 4:18-19).

The central feature of his teaching was that in him, in his words and works, the kingly reign of God had broken into human history. Demonstrating that God's absolute future was already breaking into the present, Jesus healed the sick and exorcised demons, challenged the Sabbath regulations and predicted the end of the Temple, abolished the rigid food laws and associated with the nobodies of society, pronounced God's blessing on the poor and demonstrated his presence with the persecuted, declared the forgiveness of sins, and invited the outcasts and notorious to the Kingdom banquet. All, without exception, were invited, and all, without distinction, were welcome, for this was to be a festival of grace and joy, a festival celebrating God's reign of grace.

The Kingdom is embodied in a new social reality which lives in the power of the Spirit – the Church. The central theme of the new household of God which Jesus inaugurated was grace. Forgiveness and forgivingness, acceptance and openness, and an undiscriminating love like that of God were to be its hallmark (Matt. 5: 43-48; Luke 6: 27-36). Here the least would be the greatest, the servant the ruler of all, in startling contrast with the society of this world.

At Pentecost, the New Testament Church was empowered by the Spirit to witness to the Kingdom (Acts 2:16-18), and to be an anticipation, a "first fruits" of the new creation, the sign of the final gathering together of all things into God. It was called to follow its Lord in living the Kingdom in this present age, and thus to be a bridgehead of the advancing realm of God. In Acts, we see Luke's portrayal of this Kingdom Community in the making, a community of grace. From the outset, all are accepted equally into this fellowship – irrespective of where they come from, or what they bring. In Acts 2:42-47, 4:32-35, and 5:12-18, the *koinonia* (Acts 2:42) brings together all members in prayer and table fellowship, shared suffering and common ownership of property. The believers "devoted themselves to fellowship" (Acts 2:42), "held everything in common" (Acts 2:44) and "not one of them considered anything his private property" (Acts 4:32). "There was not a needy person among them, for those who owned land or houses sold them and brought the proceeds of the sale and laid it at the apostles' feet; it was then distributed according to every individual's need" (Acts 4:34,35).

The New Testament Church sought to live out its life under the guidance of the Spirit in continuing the Kingdom attitude towards material possessions. The service of God and the sharing of life in the fellowship took priority. Their security was in God's provision through his people and all property was at the disposal of the community. Social distinctions were abolished and poverty was overcome.

Paul's letters prescribe a way of life for a community living by grace. Though there is less explicit reference to the poor or to the sharing of this world's goods in Paul's writing, 1 Corinthians 11 implies the emergence of status divisions and a consequent failure to share in the Lord's Supper. Paul calls for a society in which each looks to the good of the other, in which there is "distribution to the need of all", hospitality; and the weakest, the least, and the most deprived are given the greatest honour (1 Cor. 12).

The Church, for Paul, is itself the living expression of a grace which chooses and uses what is weak, poor, and despised in this world (1 Cor. 1:18-30). In this Church, the members are to mediate the gifts of Christ in mutual inter-dependence (1 Cor. 12, Rom. 12), in self-humiliation and self-giving (Phil. 2:5-8; 2 Cor. 8:9), and to live in anticipation of the Kingdom of God. Whenever this pattern of community appeared to be breaking down, New Testament writers comment strongly. In James there is an attack on the rich, and a pleading for the cause of poor (Jas. 1:9-11, 2:2-4, 5:1-6). 1 John 3:16-18 points to a failure in sharing as the one concrete example in the epistle about love in action.

Overall, the New Testament presents an impressive picture of the Church as the model of God's purpose for mankind. As this purpose was embodied and expressed in the life of Jesus Christ, so his followers, in the Body of Christ, continue to carry the Gospel to the world. This Gospel is proclaimed by word and deed, and the shared life of the Church is the visual aid that illustrates and conveys the grace of Christ. Changed attitudes and relationships among Christians carry through into a fundamental sharing of life at all levels. This community of grace proclaims vividly the new order of the Kingdom, transforming the lives of individuals and challenging the whole social order.

The proclamation of the "good news of the Kingdom" and its embodiment in Jesus and in the community that fully shares his life comes as a judgement on the ingrained, distorted social patterns of this world. Its values are turned upside down and its structures questioned. A new pattern is here, into which all are invited. All who hear, turn, and come in are accepted through the grace which opens up to all people this new life shared with God.

It is hard for the poor to accept this entirely unexpected invitation because of their previous exclusion from the good things of life and their relegation in the old order to the side-lines. But now they find themselves accepted and invited in first of all (Luke 4:18-19). The invitation is addressed specifically to them: "Come to me, all of you who are tired from carrying heavy loads" (Matt. 11:28). At last, the poor are able to see themselves as God created them, in their true dignity and worth. Now they are persons with something to contribute, something to share.

Just as they are inwardly healed and changed, so they are enabled to see the world through new eyes. They are no longer servants to the false structures that once threatened and trapped them. They see the central weaknesses, and know that the old patterns are already defeated and passing. In the new life of faith and the shared love of the believing community, they have fresh hope. The rich also

are summoned to discover themselves in God's sight and
to recognise that they, too, are sinners in need of grace. For
them it is much harder. They have so much they must lose
(Matt. 19:16-21). It is hard for them to receive and respond
to this invitation to live by grace, when their security lies
in wealth, power and status. It is even harder to repent and,
like Zacchaeus, to acknowledge that their wealth comes
from a defrauding of the poor. Yet the same movement of
grace can release the rich from their isolation and
estrangement.

Both those who were poor and those who were rich, on
entering into the death and risen life of Jesus Christ, find
their place together in his Kingdom community. Here
those who know themselves accepted in him, can accept
each other. Here the Magnificat is made visible. The
mighty are put down from their seats, the poor lifted up
and the hungry fed.

But those who cling to their wealth must, like the rich
young ruler, be sent away empty.

TOWARDS AN ANSWER

It is not hard to work out why we have not heard the
Scriptures on this, and on other, issues. It is uncomfortable to have our attention drawn to those who are poor for
it raises questions about equality, justice and possessions.
Those questions are sharpened when the Bible makes it
plain that, at every point, God opposes imposed poverty.
They are personalised when our own affluence is seen as
the other side of another's poverty. That creates guilt and
there are only two answers to the weight of guilt. One is to
deny or evade the truth that creates guilt, the other is
repentance and action.

In his book *Rich Man, Poor Man – and the Bible*,
Conrad Boerna maintains that poverty is no accident; it is
determined by the structures of society. Therefore poverty
is never taken for granted in the Bible. The Bible indicates
that sin, rather than nature or an evil fate, is the cause of
poverty. Poverty is never an isolated phenomenon, it is

closely connected with the social framework of a society. Boerna points out that the Bible is concerned about the poor man at three levels: the challenging of unjust structures; solidarity with the oppressed; recovery of the self-respect of the poor man. To hear this – and to heed – shifts our attitudes. We cannot be neutral, neither can we engage in a paternalistic form of charity for even the best of charity leaves unjust structures undisturbed, distances itself from the recipients and reinforces the low self-esteem of those who receive.

If the plight of the poor will not stir us into action then only the authority of the Scriptures and the example of Jesus, carrying as they do the purpose of the Creator God for His people, will effectively reach us, change us and empower us.

Signs of hope have accelerated. One is the widespread acceptance of books like *Rich Christians in an Age of Hunger* by Ronald Sider with its powerful marriage of scriptural passages and contemporary issues, followed by his *Cry Justice*, a straightforward collection of biblical material on hunger and poverty. Another is the constant request for scriptural roots and motivation answered by a wide variety of books, amongst which are *The Politics of Jesus* by John Yoder and *Poverty and Expectation in the Gospels* by David Mealand.

Another sign is the creation of communities of Christians seeking to return to the roots and to live "Kingdom-style". When this is allied to a rediscovery of the biblical wholeness we – and society – have a visual aid.

All this is part of my own journey. Others have preceded me and left markers. I owe much to the source books I have listed. I owe most to the discipline of reading right through the Bible and listening to the notes to which I had been so deaf. Digging through the quarry I have discovered the lines that run right through. I have been made to hear. To heed is another matter, and I suspect that this problem is not mine alone.

10

WAYS AHEAD

This book is written primarily for people living outside
the inner city. It is intended for those who are concerned
because of the injustice experienced by urban poor. Those
who see the "other Britain" from the vantage point of
"comfortable Britain" and acknowledge the gulf between
them. Those who follow Christ and are coloured by His
attitudes and His teaching about the individual worth of
each person.

That concern has many motivations. Compassion will
compel some towards the healing of the hurts. Others,
fired with an evangelistic zeal, will respond to the
overwhelming statistics of missionary failure and seek to
win others into a living, personal faith. Some, affronted by
the manifest injustices, will struggle with the political
issues. For others, the discovery of scriptural insights will
stimulate an examination of the discrepancy in life-styles
and our responsibility for others.

In all this complexity, what are the ways ahead? For
you, for your congregation? You can choose to ignore the
signs, to silence the cries. I can only interpret, represent
and point, hoping for an understanding and a response.

ONE VIEW

"What can *we* do, those of us who are worried about the
problem? Here are a few suggestions:

- Reduce your standard of living to Supplementary

Benefit level and give the balance to charity (you can get a leaflet from the Post Office telling you how much you would get on social security). In this way you will not only be identifying yourself with the poor but helping those in genuine need as well. Put your money where your mouth is.

- Get out and join one of the voluntary groups that is doing something practical. See for yourself what it's like. Get your hands dirty.
- Examine your own attitude. Education and a high social status doesn't give you a right to patronise those lower down the scale. Remember we are all equally sinners. Don't pretend to be more concerned than you are. If you really feel so guilty about some people being richer than others, why haven't you taken the first step in the redistribution of income yourself?
- Pray for revival. Greed, envy, worship of money breed unchecked because people see no alternative way of life in the Church. The worst poverty is not material but spiritual, and dealing with this should be the first priority of the Church. First deal with the spiritual impoverishment of Christians, then there will be something to offer the world. Obsession with politics is often a substitute for the more costly life of self-sacrifice."

(From a letter in *Third Way* September 1984, responding to an article on the Liverpool riots).

ANOTHER VIEW

- To *listen* carefully to the voice of Church people and others in Urban Priority Areas.
- To *examine* whether there are particular resistances to Christian faith and practice in these areas ("*This* Christ and *this* Church are not for us."); and why there is so much apparent indifference and so little response to present ways of proclaiming the Gospel in Urban Priority Areas.

- To *gather* information, evaluate and commend effective forms of mission and ministry; and to identify necessary developments and training in a rapidly changing society.
- To *recognise* barriers to effective working which spring from our present organisation and laws at national and diocesan level and to propose necessary changes.
- To *articulate* questions concerning public policy which arise from this enquiry.
- To *communicate* the findings in a way that will enable the whole Church to hear them and to recognise our corporate responsibility to evaluate them and to act.

(The aims of the Archbishop's Commission on Urban Priority Areas.)

STARTING THE JOURNEY

In one way or another, a journey has to begin. For those already in the inner cities or on the housing estates the first step is a recognition of the urban realities and a commitment to remain where they belong in the name of Christ. For some of those outside there will be a physical, life-committing journey that will mean a moving in, a settling among and a belonging to. That especially applies to young people who can change and blend more readily than those who are settled in home, life-style and attitudes. But it also is a direct challenge to two other groups: the professional groups who work closely with people (doctors, teachers, social workers, solicitors, ministers, nurses) and whose skills, articulateness and presence are so needed; and the couples in middle-life whose children have grown up leaving them freedom to move into the inner city for the sake of the Kingdom.

That part of the journey which is a direct relationship by residence can be life-long, a phase or a touch. Life-long, in that a deliberate decision to live in a specific locality creates a bonding, identifying reciprocity. A phase, in which for a short period of years the experience of inner city life is known, appreciated and remembered by the mobile element of the population. A touch, in which a taster course or a day visit introduces you, and continues to haunt you for life.

But the physical side of the journey will be accompanied by a mental aspect. The external experience will create an internal debate.

As so many of us have been, you will be "bugged" by the situation, wrestling with its complex symptoms, grappling with its deep significances and working towards some solution, however small. Do not fall into the trap of thinking you are the first or the only person to walk this way. Millions have lived in this struggle; the urban dilemma has been with us for at least 100 years; considerable efforts have been made by planners and politicians, and the Christian Church is one among many agencies that have entered the field. Around us and behind us are those who are fellow-workers. We can learn from them. But we have to start the journey for ourselves.

SEEING THE SITUATION

A journey opens up new horizons and takes you into fresh places. Some of the travellers have opened their eyes from their birthplace in the inner city or the council estate. Others, by reason of immigration, housing or employment, have come to live among the urban poor and have had to begin their own process of discovery. Incomers, many with religious or political motivations, have made a deliberate choice to live in the urban scene.

Two women I know who chose to live in South and East London as "incoming Christians" responded to their experience in a hymn and a poem that illustrates the seeing that is both necessary and possible.

From Camberwell in South London, a hymn written by Jane Galbraith who lives in a "hard-to-let" G.L.C. flat:

Lord of our city, we bring you its pain,
The muggings, the dole queues, the lifts bust again.

The fear of each stranger and nowhere to play,
The waiting for buses at the start of the day.

Lord of the homeless we bring you their cry,
The waiting on promises – pie in the sky –
The red tape and questions and sent on their way,
The sense of frustration at the noon of the day.

Lord of all races, all colours of skin,
Please make us fight racism, help us begin
To see how our prejudice colours the way
We treat friends and neighbours at the end of the day.

Lord of our whole lives, we bring them to you,
We're powerless, defeated 'til you make us new,
Then powered by your Spirit, we go on once more
With news of your wholeness, Good News for the poor.

From Plaistow in East London, written by Kathryn Hansford, who was then working with In-Contact Ministries:

A damp Autumn day.
Above the hustle and bustle of everyday life
The mute skyscrapers reach out to the sky
In a silent plea for salvation.
What can I offer you?
What reality can I present
In this world of pretence?
I can offer only myself
And the Jesus who is within me –
No outward miracle will change the city
But the inward miracle
Which God can work in a man's heart.
For this miracle the heart
Of the city yearns
For it is the heart which is corrupt.

Into this snakepit of sin
The love of God can penetrate.

It is with this love I reach out now,
Although I am small and the city is vast
My God is far greater than this landscape.
Weep for the city,
Weep tears of sorrow and of joy
For the Lord will work,
He will change the heart of the city
Though the landscape remains the same.

Two very different viewpoints. But two women have really
seen the situation. Their words and their insight picture
the inner city as seen by two Christians who came to stay
and to see.

GETTING BENEATH THE SURFACE

After the journey has begun and the situation has been
seen, a third level is imperative. We must get beneath the
surface. The twin dangers of superficiality and over-
simplification must be faced. The immediate answer and
the instant analysis are not the way ahead.

There has to be a mental wrestling to discover what has
happened in the past and what is going on now. There
must be a checking back over history: why did these
industrial areas come into being? What forces created
them? There needs to be a thinking-through present-day
pressures: what shapes human lives? Who controls the
power?

That will mean some hard thinking. Politically it will
mean facing up to the Marxist analysis and questioning
the generally accepted rightness of capitalism. Socially it
will mean entering into very different life-styles and
cultures. Personally, it must mean the loss of prejudice
(pre-judging) and the acceptance of sympathy.

The digging beneath the surface must be local to be real.
It is listening to local people and learning from a
distinctive situation. But the local community is bound
up inextricably with society as a whole and there has to be
an unravelling of all the influences bearing down on the
local scene.

Here are two perceptive comments about what is going on beneath the surface which should be thought about together. The first is a prophetic piece of social analysis written by David Harvey in 1973 in *Social Justice and the City:*

> Forecasting the future of an urban system requires a thorough understanding of the processes generating change and a realistic evaluation of the direction in which the Social System as a whole is being moved by these processes. I have concentrated my attention upon the mechanisms governing the redistribution of income and I have suggested that these seem to be moving towards a state of greater inequality and greater injustice. Unless this present trend can be reversed, I feel that almost certainly we are also headed for a period of intense conflict (which may be violent) within the urban system. In the United States there is enough evidence to indicate that open conflict is beginning. In Britain, the same processes are at work.

The second are some thought-provoking comments by David Wasdell of the Urban Church Project after a conference in Nottingham back in 1978. More than seventy people engaged in urban mission shared their frustrations at this conference and were reminded that:

> There is the drive to protect the institutional Church from the implications of its break-down in the inner city, both in terms of the need for renewed strategies, priorities and work within the inner city and also in terms of the implications for the structure and strategy of the Church in other areas. The inner city represents in extreme form a set of problems which are endemic throughout the western Churches and from examination of which the Church is in full flight.
> The Church is only welcome in the city provided it sustains the status quo, looks after the casualties created by the system and confirms the fundamental injustice of urban decay.

Hard words, but the way ahead does involve the facing up to the truth or otherwise of social analysis and the commentary of Christian workers living and working in the heart of the urban.

CONFRONTING THE CONSEQUENCES

Causes are one thing, consequences another. Urban deprivation, the urban poor, the two nations and "powers and powerlessness" are real, experienced consequences not sociological concepts. They affect the quality of life, determine the pattern of a human life-span and are inescapable companions well-known to many within a still affluent nation.

These consequences must be clearly seen and, whenever possible, shared. Without this, external analysis merely perpetuates the distance of detachment and we lack the motivating power that stems from the immediacy of emotion. There is no way ahead until we feel the hurt, face the anger, meet the bitterness and experience for ourselves the frustrations. Racism is understood when a black man shares his feelings; poverty becomes real when a single-parent mother takes you through her budget; unemployment is more than statistics when a teenager talks tonelessly about "the system".

When the consequences are confronted two changes will occur. The first has to do with dimension, the second with attitude. The sheer scale of the urban priority areas, their long-standing roots in history and the relative failure of human efforts brings home the dimension of the problem. This can be seen in economic terms but beneath it all lurks the deeper issue of justice set against the recognition of structural sin linked with the "principalities and powers" at work in the dark places of our society. Alongside our dawning recognition of the dimensions runs a changing of inner attitudes. Our quick judgments falter as we see that most human poverty is created by social, economic and spiritual forces far greater than individual fecklessness or stupidity. Our immediate response in charitable giving withers as we understand that this is but a poultice on the symptoms and no cure for the disease.

But when we begin to express all this, another and surprising consequence will speedily surface. Angry reaction from those we considered to be our families and friends, accusations of "going left" or accepting "the social Gospel" from colleagues, and the pursed lips and silent withdrawal of those who fear the application of the new understanding. This reaction must be expected and faced by all who confront the consequences of urban poverty and through their changed convictions and concern speak out from within the urban situation to their friends who look on from the outside.

MAKING THE WORD FLESH

The double command of Jesus Christ to Christians to "go into the world" and "preach the Good News to the poor" has not been countermanded. Our generation is not the first to wrestle with the task of "making the Word flesh" in its own time.

In the past urban mission thrusts, the Good News has been fleshed in the buildings, the programmes and the people of the Church. Their very presence, involvement, commitment, love and adventuring spirit runs through the British urban scene like words through a stick of rock. Break it at any point and the message, however smudged or weak, is there.

The way ahead today means learning both from their failures and their insights. The initiative of individuals, the difficulties over authentic identification, the perpetuation of a colony, the failure to get beyond symptoms to causes and the constant weakness of doing things *for* instead of *with* are the product of our class-conscious society and a fundamental weakness in the light of scriptural patterns. The valid insights we have received include those of presence (parish and priest), social caring, evangelistic effort and continuity within ministry.

Making the Word flesh today for those who live on our
vast council estates or within the inner cities will mean a
going and a giving. There is no alternative to incarnation.
The "shooting star" concept of a sudden, bright, rapid
burn-out ministry is inappropriate. There has to be a
burial in the situation before ministry can begin. The
hidden years of Jesus that preceded the public ministry
have their parallel within urban mission. The invitation
of the London music-hall song, "The Lambeth Walk":
"Why don't you make your way there?/Go there, stay
there..." has to be answered physically and totally. Where
that happens the Good News is proclaimed and the
Kingdom comes. The Gospel has to become visible before
it is audible.

For Jesus this meant birth in Bethlehem, life in Nazareth,
and death on Calvary. For Paul it was the prayer that "I
may know the fellowship of his sufferings and the power
of his resurrection". For us it has a message at many levels.
Those who are already earthed in the urban scene have to
ask whether that identification and natural acceptance
should not be continued that the Word might be made
flesh – and that raises serious questions about the assumed
rightness of moving out and away to the "better areas".
Those who are outside the urban areas need to ask whether
they can become the incomers, the "scaffolding" that
allows a new building to rise, the "seed that falls into the
ground" and that will demand a settling-in, a hidden
phase, and a setting-aside of status and achievement
values. Those who are outside and cannot physically enter
the housing estates and the inner city have the task of
discerning and supporting by encouragement, prayer and
resources, those groups and individuals which are
authentic and committed to making the Word flesh.

For those who consider themselves "called to the
ministry" this will mean an answer to the puzzled
question of the inner city churches: "why are we so often
the last place a clergyman wants to come to?" If the road
leads on there will have to be a time of induction to allow

understanding and appreciation of the values and the struggles of the new culture. There will certainly be a questioning of the usual "king of the castle" approach of the theological student. Some inner city people who have the vocation for leadership have already turned away from what they call the "starching process" of theological training and are preparing themselves in the context, training within their own culture and setting their thinking alongside their experience.

But the real weight of urban mission must be borne by the members of a new urban order now clearly seen at work within the urban priority areas. Indigenous and incomer, black and white, women and men; breaking across the barriers of denomination, culture and education, and the lay-ministerial divide; they share a sense of calling and concern as they struggle to embody and make visible the eternal World of salvation and reconciliation they have received within themselves. In this new order, incarnation precedes proclamation, proclamation is earthed and verbal, the verbal is both the listening to the city cries and the "naming of the Name".

Pip Wilson, a youth leader at the Mayflower Family Centre, set out some of the feelings and questions involved in a personal response:

People say, "No conversions? No Christians?"
People say, "You can't just love people!"
People say, "Starting where people are at is *not enough*. What about *sin*, conversions? What about preaching the straight message of Salvation? What about . . . ?"
Perhaps I should not work with kids I see in the gutters.
Perhaps if I aimed for those who would respond, we would get more results? There *are* others who are able to respond differently than our kids.
But who would handle the kids in the gutter?
Who else would take them in?
Who else would cater for their very basic needs?
They demand so much attention, their needs are so very great.

I know eternal life *is* important! Vital!
Jesus came to make it possible! It cost!
All that is available to our kinds and I know it is
important to be proclaimers of this good news.

Perhaps I should leave here and take that Youth Leader
job at Sudbury-on-Thames?
Then I would have the satisfaction of an active
fellowship, conversions and growth.
But what would happen to the kids around here?

DISCERNING EMERGING PATTERNS

Signs of hope are everywhere, whether they be strong and
obvious or hidden and little known. The way ahead is to
discover what is happening, check the signs against the
scriptural basis, and then to realise our task is "To work at,
and not to work out, the purpose of God."
    This can be done practically by:

- Linking up with committed groups and networks –
  national groups like Jubilee, C.O.S.P.E.C., E.C.U.M.,
  U.T.U. and others listed under the resources section.
- Reading the developing literature – whether that be
  magazines like *City Cries* or *Third Way* or the wave of
  books and publications which have been referred to and
  are listed under resources.
- Following a theme. Working at the issues and discovering those already tackling the problem. Whether that be
  racism (C.A.R.A.F. and Zebra) or poverty (Church
  Action against Poverty) or unemployment (Church
  Action with the Unemployed) – a list of names and
  addresses follow.
- Getting into the switchboards – as in the discovery of
  community groups drawn together in N.A.C.C.A.N.
  and the associated magazine communities. The *Directory of Christian Groups, Communities and Networks*
  is a mine of information.
- Supporting by prayer, understanding and money those
  who are working at the interface.

This will lead to a growing acceptance of the diverse nature of the signs of hope matching the needs of the urban kaleidoscope. It will mean facing a backlash of reaction at many levels as vested interests, within and outside the Church, political extremists, and sectional outlooks, both in sect and denomination – all come together to oppose, deride or sidetrack. It indicates a realisation that many of the signs of hope are transitional – interim Churches and groups moving towards a more total, complete Kingdom picture. But it could also mean that we are experiencing, in Alan Ecclestone's phrase, "the dawn chorus of a new creation."

We are on the edge of a new movement that is not afraid to make the meaning of biblical faith specific to circumstances, both personal and public. Something is happening, in spite of our human jealousies and imperfections. A new pattern is emerging, struggling free from the constraints of the past.

To sense that, to work for that, and to rejoice in that is the way ahead. It will mean change. Change in the biblical sense of conversion. Whether that be in the progressive experience of conversion to Christ, the Church and the World, or in the conversion to faith and action set out by Jim Wallis in *The Call to Conversion:*

> The goal of biblical conversion is not to save souls apart from history but to bring the Kingdom of God into the world with explosive force; it begins with individuals but is for the sake of the world. The more strongly present that goal is, the more genuinely biblical a conversion is. Churches today are tragically split between those who stress conversion but have forgotten its goal, and those who emphasise Christian social action but have forgotten the necessity for conversion. Today's converts need their eyes opened to history as much as today's activists need their spirit opened to conversion. But first, both need to recover the original meaning of conversion to Jesus Christ and to his Kingdom. Only then can our painful division be healed and the integrity of the Church's proclamation be

restored. Only then can we be enabled to move beyond
the impasse that has crippled and impoverished the
Churches for so long.

HEARING AND HEEDING THE SCRIPTURES

It is difficult to begin the way ahead and impossible to
continue without a sense of the dynamic thrust and
undergirding strength of God's purpose seen in Jesus
Christ and set out in the Bible. The recent emphasis in
urban mission practice and writing on the centrality of the
Scriptures is much wider than the evangelical world.
Activism is not enough.

The way ahead for the whole Church will mean a
freshness of hearing and an acceptance of the implications
of great biblical themes like Jubilee, *Shalom* and Justice.
It will mean a holding together of the two-edged mission
of evangelism and social justice. It will mean a new life-
style modelled on the Book of Acts (they had all things in
common) and the Epistles (the Body of Christ).

In his book *Poverty, Revolution and the Church*, Michael
Paget-Wilkes answers his question "Where do we go from
here?" by maintaining that obedience to the scriptures
will mean:

A new example by the Church to Society. This begins
with repentance. It continues with the working-out of a
new medium within the structures, wealth and buildings of the Church.

Changes in the Church's relationship to Society. This
means refusal to give blanket support to the attitudes
and institutions of an imperfect and often corrupt
society. It will go on to the discovery of methods of
changing society.

New patterns of ministry. These must include identification with the needy, the erosion of false values
(status), a new agenda, the emancipation of the

oppressed, and personal and corporate changes.

The rediscovery of the wholeness of biblical truth is one of the most significant signs of the Spirit in the cities. This gives a perspective, an authority and a vision that has to precede and then accompany any urban pilgrimage. It is a constant reminder of the initiative of God, the goal of His Kingdom and the Gifts of the Spirit to be set alongside our daily preoccupations, self-centredness and dependence on human leadership.

FOLLOW THE SIGNS

There is an ancient Christian legend, popularised in a book and a film entitled *Quo Vadis?* In the story, the apostle Peter flees from the city of Rome along the Appian Way. On his way out of the city he meets Jesus going in. "Quo Vadis, Domine?" (Where are you going, Master?) is his question. "I go to the city in your stead," comes the answer. Peter hesitates, turns and goes back to the city to die – a witness and a sign.

It is a powerful, haunting legend which has stayed with me since I first heard it. It dramatically sets out the experienced tension between Christ's way and our human inclinations. It graphically reminds us that the word disciple means follower. It points beyond itself to the spiritual realities of losing to find, of dying to live, and of giving to receive. It holds together the city, the disciples and Christ.

It has been an incredibly rich experience for me to have lived through a succession of signs. They have been guides. They point on. They sum up in themselves both the earthiness and the eternity of the Gospel. They root back to the scriptural patterns and beckon towards the glory that has yet to be revealed.

When Trevor Huddleston became the Anglican Bishop of Stepney local people made two comments: "He's the first Bishop of Stepney ever to live in Stepney" and "He lives down our street." The fact that previous Bishops of

Stepney lived in the leafy suburb of Loughton had been noted as one sign. The change of address was a very different sign.

Committed groups have sprung up. Whether it be the Urban Training Unit led by John Vincent in Sheffield or the Urban Mission Programme pioneered by Donald Reeves in London; whether it be the Youth Leaders drawn together by the Frontier Youth Trust or the radical activists under the banner of C.O.S.P.E.C.; whether it be the Anglo-Catholic Jubilee or the evangelical E.U.P.T. – everywhere you look there are indications of thought, action and discipleship in the cities.

New congregations are springing up within and around our cities, long-established churches have known their own death-resurrection experience. I can take you to once redundant churches now alive with a freshly planted congregation or vibrant with a black Church in worship. You can see the seeds of life in the missionary organisations and the church-planting agencies.

You will meet signs in the wave of associations, projects and programmes that address themselves to a specific urban issue. The list is endless, indicating a rising tide of committed and practical response.

You will discover signs in the inter-Church world of denominations. The Methodist Mission Alongside the Poor with publications like *What Churches can do* and the Archbishop of Canterbury's Commission on Urban Priority Areas due to report in 1985 are matched by initiatives and concern among the U.R.C.s, Baptists and Roman Catholics.

You will see signs in the even wider world of Government and social concern. The Scarman Report, the Urban Programme, and the political debate on metropolitan boroughs and rate-capping all point to the social struggle for justice that is a Kingdom concern.

You will be overwhelmed by the signs carried in the literature and writings. From pathfinding books like Bishop Wickham's *Church and People in an Industrial City*, to the contemporary titles of *Urban Harvest; Bias to the Poor; Starting All Over Again; Poverty, Revolution and the Church; Scandal of Poverty*. From magazines like *Christians in Industrial Areas* to the new format *City Cries*. But above all in the increasing stress on the scriptural.

In the following of the signs the journey begins, and there will be baton-passing as the pioneer runners complete their phase and pass on the responsibility to others. On that journey we will understand again who He is and what He expects.

He's a friend of the poor, and he brings good news;
A friend of the oppressed, he walks in their shoes.
He marches for justice and new-born truths;
He's the healer of the broken, confused and abused.
And those of us who follow him, must walk in his shoes.

WHEREVER YOU LOOK

Signposts and signs abound: in the social and political struggles, in renewed congregations and emerging networks, in concerned and committed individuals. In all the churches and at every level there is evidence of a wrestling with reality and a response that is both earthed and expressed.

From Merseyside, a Roman Catholic priest writes honestly and powerfully in *Passion for the Inner City*:

When I came to the Inner City I had a desire eventually to speak of new formats of ministry and religious life, but it was the unexpected which took over. I became exposed to an experience which shattered my institutional and structural mind and will. It was not the powerlessness or poverty situation which did this directly, it was the wonder of the human being staying alive in the midst of all this. Yet this wonder of humanity which faced me also highlighted the sinfulness of a situation which human beings had to face day in and day out. In evangelical terms, having gone to minister to the least of the brethren, the least of the brethren ministered to us.[1]

In Bradford, a group of Baptists from all the city congregations met in conference to look at ministry. They walked through their own districts to see what was happening. One of them, Dilys Peacock, jotted down the results in the form of a prayer:

Lord, we looked at the areas around our churches and saw signs of care and neglect; signs of love and hate; signs of progress and decay; signs of hope and despair; signs of tolerance and intolerance.

Around Westgate there was the multi-racial football match and bilingual shop signs, welcoming signs at the church and new housing. But there was also damp housing, dereliction and a prostitute with her client.

Around Tetley Street there were signs of a multi-racial community with groups for English and Asians at the church, shops owned by Hindus and Muslims, Polish and Ukrainian clubs and Muslim and Christian symbols on house doors. We saw improvement areas, C.N.D. and anti-racist signs and noted that a new "Inter-Link" centre is to open. But here were also areas littered with rubbish, a wall mural saying "Lesbians are everywhere" and teenage girls coming out of the local pub.

In Girlington we saw signs of urban renewal with a new school, health centre plus family centre, areas of landscaping and new housing for the elderly and small families. We saw the advice centre and community centre attached to the Methodist-Baptist church and signs of a mixed community with Asian corner shops. But there was also vandalism with the church windows smashed, litter and only one phone-box working.

In Bowling there were more signs of urban renewal with landscaping, road improvement and new housing and signs of a multi-racial area in the Asian shops. We saw a community centre and some thriving churches.

But we also saw graffiti-covered subways under the busy dual carriageways.

Lord, we thank you for all the signs of tolerance, caring, loving and sharing that we have seen in the neighbourhoods around our Churches. We ask you to help us, as individuals and Churches, to face up to the challenges presented by the signs of intolerance, neglect, hatred and despair and to do all we can to reflect your love in Bradford.[2]

At a much wider level the World Council of Churches at Vancouver in 1984 saw "witnessing among the poor" as a special area of concern in the debate on mission and evangelism. Sections and a prayer from that report set "Signs in the City" in a world and personal context:

The Church is called to witness to the Good News of the life, death and resurrection of Jesus Christ, to a world where there is a frightening and growing gap between rich and poor nations and between rich and poor within nations. Poverty exists on an unprecedented global scale.

In a world which is today torn by conflicting ideologies, the poor are most apt to be ignored and forgotten. An increasing number of people find themselves marginalised, second-class citizens unable to control their own destiny and resigned to being and remaining poor. Children, the disabled, and women are among those who suffer most seriously the cruelty and despair of poverty.

Poverty is treated as a problem, rather than as a scandal calling for radical action to attack its causes and roots in human sinfulness and unwillingness to share.

The message of the prophets is that God in no way assumes a neutral position between the rich and the poor. God is on the side of the poor and champions their cause for justice and fullness of life.

In not sharing the good news of the Gospel there has been a double injustice; the poor are victims of social, economic and political oppression and often have been deprived of the knowledge of God's special love for them and the energising liberation which such knowledge brings. In the parable of the Last Judgement (Matt. 25:31ff) Jesus identifies himself with the hungry, the homeless, the naked, the sick and prisoners. This demands of us as Christians a corresponding allegiance. If we are to follow Christ then we must care for the poor and seek to reverse their situation.

The Church's call to witness in the life of the poor is therefore a call for the people of God to rethink priorities in missions and programmes, and it is a challenge to life-style on both a corporate and individual level. A more simple life-style and even a life of poverty is laid on the Church and Christians as a witness to the poverty of Christ "who though he was rich for our sake became poor" (2 Cor. 8:9). Christians and Churches, of course, find themselves in very different circumstances, some rich and others poor. To all, the call to share the good news with the poor comes as a priority and a specific challenge. The Gospel must be proclaimed in both word and deed; word without service is empty and service without the word is without power. The Churches today are learning afresh, through the call to witness to the poor, to overcome the old dichotomy between evangelism and social action.

We rejoice that the churches are growing today among the poor of the earth and that new insights and perspectives on the Gospel are coming to the whole Church from communities of the poor. They are discovering and making known dimensions of the Gospel which have long been neglected and forgotten by the Church. The richness and freshness of their experience is an inspiration, blessing and challenge to the established churches.

Lord God our Father,
look with mercy upon us;
forgive our indifference to cries of need
and our blindness to the signs of your kingdom.
Speak to us your word of truth and enable us to hear.
Open for us the way of life and strengthen us to
    follow.
Set before us the love of Christ and make us true
    disciples.
For your name's sake. Amen.[3]

11
SIGNPOSTS

This is an integral part of *Signs in the City*, not merely an appendix of addresses and books. Here are some signposts for the journey. They provide possible indicators for different routes, for we live in separate parts of the country, know ourselves to be at individual points on our pilgrimage, and are involved with different issues.

The signposts are selective. There is now such a wealth of indicators and initiatives that some of us are going over to computer!

It is a personal compilation with omissions and biases that you are bound to observe. But you have to start somewhere and the persistent will discover the uncharted roads.

Wherever possible the groups and agencies are given dates and the book-list is in chronological order. This indicates both the unfolding and the acceleration of urban mission in the U.K.

NETWORKS

Networks have grown up to cover the whole country. Each has its own emphasis and style and most have their own publications. They include:
AFRO-WEST INDIAN UNITED COUNCIL OF
CHURCHES   1976
The Centre for Caribbean Studies, 76 Bridport Place,
London, N1 5DS
01-729 0986

Ecumenical but mainly Pentecostal churches.
West Indian Concern
Directory

CHRISTIAN ORGANISATIONS FOR SOCIAL, POLITICAL AND ECONOMIC CHANGE

C.O.S.P.E.C.   1980
c/o Lambeth Mission, 1-5 Lambeth Road, London,
SE1 7DQ
01-735 2166
Federation of groups and movements committed to the
struggle for a just, participatory and sustainable society.
C.O.S.P.E.C. Bulletin

EVANGELICAL COALITION FOR URBAN
MISSION   1980
Scripture Union House, 130 City Road, London,
EC1V 2NJ
01-250 1966
Coalition of Evangelical Christians for Racial Justice,
Evangelical Urban Training Project, Frontier Youth
Trust and Shaftesbury Project (Inner City Group).
City Cries

JUBILEE GROUP   1974
St. Clement's House, Sirdar Road, London, W.11
01-727 5450
Network of Christians, mainly within the Anglican
Catholic tradition and within the socialist movement.

NATIONAL CENTRE FOR CHRISTIAN
COMMUNITIES AND NETWORKS   1981
Westhill College, Weoley Park Road, Birmingham,
B29 6LL
021 472 8079
Meeting point and resource for Christian groups, com-
munities and networks.
Community
Directory - with nearly 400 groups listed.

DENOMINATIONS AND AGENCIES

All denominations and agencies, at varying levels, are now concerned with urban mission. Departments of Mission or Social Responsibility can connect you. But some, by tradition or contemporary development, are deeply involved. They include:

CATHOLIC SOCIAL WELFARE COMMISSION
1A Stert Street, Abingdon, Oxon OX14 3JL
Wide brief and literature on all social issues. *Good News for the Poor. Church and City Problems* is useful.

CHURCH ARMY   1882
Independents Road, London, SE3 9LG
01-318 1226
Anglican action arm often working in inner cities.

METHODIST HOME MISSION DIVISION   1856
1 Central Buildings, London SW1H 9EH
01-222 8010
Through 'Mission Alongside the Poor' is working at urban mission. *Two Nations, One Gospel* and *What Churches can do* are good, cheap (50p) pamphlets.

SALVATION ARMY   1865
101 Queen Victoria Street, London, EC4 4EP.
01-236 5222
Long-term inner city involvement, particularly in social care.

ISSUE-CENTRED GROUPS

There is a wide, almost bewildering array of these that range from traditional to contemporary and they cover almost all aspects of urban society.

A. LINKING EVANGELISM AND SOCIAL ACTION.
Two out of many examples are:

SHAFTESBURY SOCIETY 1844
Shaftesbury House, 2A, Amity Grove, Raynes Park, London SW20 0LJ
01-946 6635
A long-established agency bringing "good news" in word and deed.

CORNERSTONE 1980
Cornerstone House, 5 Ethel Street, Birmingham B2 4BG
021-632 5136
New network of centres linking evangelism and social action through "coffee houses" and "alternatives to pubs".

B. EVANGELISM AND CHURCH PLANTING
For long carried by the denominations, then agencies like the Church Army, the Salvation Army and the City Missions. The new Churches now stress church planting. Two examples are:

ICHTHUS TEAM MINISTRIES 1975
Ichthus House, 116 Perry Vale, London, SE23 2IQ
01-291 4057
Blending church planting, evangelism, Bible teaching and social action.

IN-CONTACT MINISTRIES 1980
St. Andrews Road, London, E13 8QD
01-474 0743
Training and action, particularly among the ethnic groupings.

C. COMMUNITY CONCERN
Many churches have their own Boards of Social Responsibility or Community Work Sections.
A full reference point can be obtained from Local Councils of Social Services or:

NATIONAL COUNCIL FOR VOLUNTARY ORGANISATIONS
26 Bedford Square, London, WC1B 3HU
01-636 4066
Two examples of Christian involvement at community development and research level are:

AVEC 1976
155A Kings Road, London, SW3 5TX
01-352 2033
A service agency for Church and community work.

LIVERPOOL INSTITUTE OF SOCIO-RELIGIOUS STUDIES 1966
Christ's and Notre Dame College, Wooltan Road, Liverpool L16 8ND
051-722 7331
R.C. research in religious and educational sociology and social work.

D. HOUSING
A massive involvement through housing associations is a feature of the last twenty years. Details can be obtained from denominations or:

NATIONAL FEDERATION OF HOUSING ASSOCIATIONS
30 Southampton Street, London, WC2
01-240 2771

E. POLITICS
There are many Christian/political groupings but three very different signposts are:

IONA COMMUNITY 1938
The Abbey, Iona, Argyll PA76 6SN
068 17 404
Scottish-based, ecumenical renewal approach always concerned with urban/industrial areas.

CORRYMEELA COMMUNITY 1965
8 Upper Crescent, Belfast BT7 1NT
0232 225008
A community of reconciliation and renewal in Church
and society in N. Ireland.

POLITICS AND FORGIVENESS PROJECT 1983
3/35 Buckingham Gate, London SW1
01-828 2483
Exploring forgiveness and politics in the processes of
group life.

F. POVERTY
Facts and figures from:

CHILD POVERTY ACTION GROUP
1 Macklin Street, London, WC2
01-242 9149

LOW PAY UNIT
9 Poland Street, London W1V 3DG
01-437 1780

Christian response in:

CHURCH ACTION ON POVERTY 1982
27 Blackfriars Road, Salford, Greater Manchester, M3
7AQ
061-832 7815
Area based groups considering the theology and ideology
underlying poverty.

WILLIAM TEMPLE FOUNDATION 1947
Manchester Business School, Manchester M15 6PB
061-273-8228
Promoting Christian social thought and practice in urban
society – especially in industry, poverty, and community
work.

G. RACISM
Black and white partnership is emerging across the country through groups like:

CENTRE FOR BLACK AND WHITE CHRISTIAN PARTNERSHIP   1977
Selly Oak Colleges Library Extension, Bristol Road, Birmingham B29 6LQ
021-472 7952
Meeting-point, resource centre and courses.

ZEBRA PROJECT   1975
1 Merchant Street, London, E3 4LY
01-980 3745
Bringing together black and white Churches in a race-relations project.

Groups concerned with race relations, racial justice and the difficulties/opportunities of a pluralistic society have sprung up in every section of the Church:

CHRISTIANS AGAINST RACISM AND FASCISM   1978
119 East India Dock Road, London E14 6DE
01-987 6851

COMMUNITY AND RACE RELATIONS UNIT
British Council of Churches, 2 Eaton Gate, London SW1W 9BL
01-730 9611

EVANGELICAL CHRISTIANS FOR RACIAL JUSTICE   1972
12 Bell Barn Shopping Centre, Birmingham B15 2DZ
021 622 6807

CATHOLIC ASSOCIATION FOR RACIAL JUSTICE
5 Henry Road, London N4 2LH
01-800 6148

Those concerned about the multi-faith dimension will
find help from:
MULTI-FAITH RESOURCE UNIT   1982
1 College Walk, Bristol Road, Selly Oak, Birmingham
B29 6LE
021 472 0139

H. UNEMPLOYMENT

Again, most denominations now have action groups but
two very different emphases are carried by:

CHURCH ACTION WITH THE
UNEMPLOYED   1982
146 Queen Victoria Street, London, EC4V 4BY
01-236 8430
Puts you in touch with local contact people. Good leaflets.

BRITISH UNEMPLOYMENT RESOURCES
NETWORK
318 Summer Lane, Birmingham B19 3RL
021 359 3562

I. YOUTH

FRONTIER YOUTH TRUST   1964
Scripture Union House, 130 City Road, London
EC1V 2NJ
01-250 1966
Evangelically based network of Christian youth workers,
especially in urban industrial areas.

TRAINING

Those outside and inside the urban priority areas are now
offered many forms of training:

EVANGELICAL URBAN TRAINING PROJECT 1969
P.O. BOX 83 Liverpool L69 8AN
051 709 1463
Lay training workshops for urban mission aiming
especially at working class Christians.

URBAN MINISTRY PROJECT   1969
St. James Rectory, 197 Piccadilly, London W1V 9LF
01 734 4511
Situational and analytical – mainly for professionals.

URBAN THEOLOGY UNIT   1969
Pitsmoor Study House, 210 Abbeyfield Road, Sheffield
S4 7AZ
0742 388035
Linking many projects. Publications, courses.

On an ever wider basis institutes and centres are springing
up in many cities, usually offering courses and research.
Examples are:

**LONDON INSTITUTE FOR CONTEMPORARY
CHRISTIANITY**   1982
St. Peter's Church, Vere Street, London, W1M 9HP
01-629 3615
Lay institute to help Christians relate faith to life.

**OXFORD INSTITUTE FOR CHURCH AND
SOCIETY**   1975
303, Cowley Road, Oxford
0865 723085
Exploring faith/social issues arising from industrial/
pluralist society.

OXFORD CENTRE FOR MISSION STUDIES   1983
P.O. BOX 70, Woodstock Road, Oxford
0865 56071
Linking Third World and U.K.

SHAFTESBURY PROJECT   1967
8 Oxford Street, Nottingham, NG1 5BH
0602 470876
Education and research on Christian social involvement.

PUBLICATIONS

Many, and increasing, but those with application to urban mission are:

AUDENSHAW FOUNDATION 1964
2 Eaton Gate, London SW1W 9BL
01-730 9611
International clearing house for information about laity projects.

CHRISTIAN ACTION JOURNAL 1947
St. Peter's House, 308, Kennington Lane, London, SE11 5HY
01-735 2372
Promoting Christian principles and racial justice in public life.

C.O.S.P.E.C. BULLETIN
CITY CRIES } See under NETWORKS
COMMUNITY

EXODUS
404 Kingsland Road, London E8
From the black Churches

GRASS ROOTS
57 Dorchester Road, Lytchett Minster, Poole, Dorset BH16 6JE
0202 631704
Published by Post Green Community – aiming to be a force for renewal in the Church and in society and to be a friend to the poor and the oppressed.

ONE FOR CHRISTIAN RENEWAL 1970
19 Steventon Road, London, W12 0SX
01-743 4917
Folder about renewal of Church and society.

BOOKS

The list is accelerating. Bibliographies can be obtained from the networks.

With great discipline I have selected 10 only! Their titles and dates indicate the growing concern and response within urban mission. Each has been a milestone in my own journey.

Church and People in an Industrial City. E. Wickham, Lutterworth, 1957

Culture, Class and Christian Beliefs, John Benington, Scripture Union, 1973

Built as a City, David Sheppard, Hodder and Stoughton, 1974

Urban Ghetto, Douglas Bartles-Smith and David Gerrard, Lutterworth, 1976

Starting All Over Again, John Vincent, World Council cf Churches, 1981

Poverty, Revolution and the Church, Michael Paget-Wilkes, Paternoster, 1981

Urban Harvest, Roy Joslin, Evangelical Press, 1982

Bias to the Poor, David Sheppard, Hodder and Stoughton, 1983

Towards the Recovery of a Lost Bequest, Roger Dowley, ECUM, 1983

People, Churches and Multi-Racial Projects, Tony Holden, Methodist Church, 1984

NOTES

Chapter 1
1. *World View 1985*, Pluto Press, 1984.
2. Jacques Ellul, *The Presence of the Kingdom*, S.C.M., 1948.

Chapter 3
1. Charles Booth, *Life and Labour of the People in London*, Macmillan, 1902.
2. Peter Shore, M.P., quoted in *London, we're staying here*, G.L.C., 1977, p.1.
3. John Mills, *The Guardian*, Economic Extra, 12.11.1979.
4. *To Hear and to Heed*, Urban Bishops Coalition (U.S.A.) Forward Movement, 1978, p.43.
5. R. Kennedy-Cox, *Through the Dock Gates*, Michael Joseph, 1939, p.34.

Chapter 4
1. Charles Booth, *Life and Labour of the People in London*, Third Series, Religious Influences, Macmillan, 1902, vol. 7, ch. 10, para. 1.
2. Horace Mann, from comments on the 1851 Census, quoted by K.S. Inglis, *Churches and the Working Classes in Victorian England*, Routledge and Kegan Paul, 1963, p.20.
3. Nicholas Stacey, *Who Cares?* Hodder and Stoughton, 1971, p.77.
4. *Stratford Express*, 7.1.1933.
5. K. S. Inglis, *Churches and the Working Classes in Victorian England*, Routledge and Kegan Paul, 1963, p.195.
6. *Stratford Express*, 24.1.1920.

Chapter 5
1. Peter Townsend, *Poverty in the U.K.*, Pelican, 1979.
2. *Christian Witness to the Urban Poor*, Lausanne Committee for World Evangelisation, 1980, p.7.
3. Benjamin Disraeli, *Sybil*, book iv, ch. 8.
4. Ruth Glass, "Urban Sociology in Great Britain", a trend report published in *Current Sociology*, vol. *IV*, no. 4, 1955.

Chapter 6
 1. E. Wickham, *Church and People in an Industrial City*,
    Lutterworth, 1957.
 2. From the Audenshaw Papers.
 3. Tom Allan, *The Face of my Parish*, S.C.M., 1954, p.11.
 4. John Vincent, *Starting All Over Again*, W.C.C., 1981.
 5. Maisie Ward, *France Pagan*, Sheed and Ward, 1949.
 6. Bruce Kenrick, *Come out the Wilderness*, Fontana, 1962.
 7. Harvey Cox, *Secular City*, S.C.M., 1965.
 8. Gibson Winter, *Suburban Captivity of the Churches*,
    Macmillan, 1962.
 9. Greg Smith and David Driscoll, *West Ham Church Survey*,
    E.C.U.M., 1984.
10. Peter Brierley, *Prospect for the Eighties*, Bible Society, 1979.
11. John Pellow, *The Concrete Village*, Hodder and Stoughton,
    1967, p.36.

Chapter 7
 1. *Directory of Christian groups, communities and networks*,
    available from N.A.C.C.A.N., Westhill College, Selly Oak,
    Birmingham 29.
 2. Roswith Gerloff, *Partnership in Black and White*, Methodist
    Church, 1977.

Chapter 8
 1. From the aims of the Archbishop of Canterbury's Com-
    mission on Urban Priority Areas. Set up in 1983 and due to
    report late 1985.
 2. Andrew Busby in the Cann Hall Baptist Church Newsletter,
    October 1983.
 3. David Watson.

Chapter 10
 1. Austin Smith, *Passion for the Inner City*, Sheed and Ward,
    1983, p.73.
 2. Dilys Peacock at a Central Bradford Baptist Fellowship
    Conference in March 1985, under the title "Called to...?"
 3. Extracts from the report of the World Council of Churches
    Assembly in Vancouver 1984, published, together with the
    prayer, by Methodists Alongside the Poor in leaflet M.A.P. 2.